STILL SEARCHING FOR PIPE DREAMS

STILL SEARCHING
FOR PIPE DREAMS

Rick Newcombe

Sumner Books
Hermosa Beach

Copyright © 2012, 2013 by Rick Newcombe

Sumner Books
737 3rd St.
Hermosa Beach, CA 90254
ISBN 978-1-939104-03-8

THIRD PRINTING

Rick Newcombe's email address: rnewcombe@creators.com

Printed in the United States of America

To my mother and father, Ann and Leo Newcombe, who always encouraged me to pursue my pipe dreams.

~~~~~

CONTENTS

~~~ BONUS CHAPTERS ~~~

STILL SEARCHING
FOR PIPE DREAMS

CHAPTER ONE

A QUIET REVOLUTION

Norman Rockwell's "Triple Self-Portrait" shows us a man who clearly identifies himself as a pipe smoker.

Imagine discovering a secret treasure that could transform your life. That is how I feel about pipe collecting and moderate pipe smoking (without inhaling), as I explained in this first chapter, which I wrote for a presentation to the Seattle Pipe Club in January 2008.

This book is a continuation of my first book, "In Search of Pipe Dreams," in which I reprint articles and speeches that I have written for pipe publications and pipe groups, as well as presenting some new material. My writings have never sought to offer a definitive account or history of the pipe business, nor is there anything in them that even remotely resembles what an art critic does.

Instead, I offer my highly opinionated observations about this unique and eccentric hobby, in a first-person voice. Over the years I have received far more encouragement and praise for these writings than I ever could have hoped to imagine. At the same time, some of my fellow collectors were occasionally upset by my writings. I regret that, because in the end, regardless of our differing opinions, if you love your pipes, then we are united by a bond that is very strong and quite unique in the world today.

* * * * *

There is a brilliant pipe maker in Japan named Kei Gotoh. Along with the legendary Tokutomi and several others, Kei Gotoh is considered one of the best pipe sculptors of all time. And I particularly like him because he paid me the most peculiar compliment when we first met.

It was at the Chicago Pipe Show a few years ago, and he was with other Japanese pipe makers, several of whom were dressed in traditional black kimonos with Tabi socks and woven slippers, their long hair tied in a bun. After we were introduced, Kei Gotoh bowed and said, "Ah, Mr. Newcombe, it is such an honor to meet you. I love your book. It is on my nightstand, and you put me to sleep every night!"

Well, I hope I won't put you to sleep with my reflections

on pipe smoking past, present and future.

I want to explore the issue of why any of us would still smoke a pipe in the 21st century when it is viewed as such an unusual thing to do, to say the least. There are even some people who regard it as dangerous and irresponsible, and if they had their way, it would be classified as a criminal activity. At best, society views pipe smoking today as a hopelessly eccentric and out-of-date pastime completely at odds with modern manners, opinion and decorum.

It wasn't always this way. In fact, pipe smoking has been popular for many centuries. In the United States, our country has its roots in tobacco. George Washington was a tobacco farmer and John Adams a pipe smoker. During the American Civil War of the 1860s, soldiers on both sides were frequently photographed with pipes in their mouths. Our earliest images of Santa Claus showed a jolly man with a clay pipe. During the roaring twenties most college men, and their professors, were pipe smokers. Then came the Great Depression of the 1930s, when the pipe was the poor man's way to smoke because you only need one or two inexpensive pipes to smoke, and pipe tobacco lasts a long time. Following World War II, the pipe was pictured with television and movie fathers in one show after another, including with Spencer Tracy in the original movie version of Father of the Bride. It is not surprising that The Washington Post once called pipe smoke "the aroma of fatherhood."

Norman Rockwell, a lifetime pipe smoker, was arguably the most popular American artist and illustrator of the 20th century, and his 322 cover paintings for The Saturday Evening Post have become legendary. One of his most famous paintings is his triple self-portrait, in which he is studying his face in a mirror and showing us the canvas on which he is painting, while we see the whole picture as if we were standing behind the artist. In the portrait on the canvas, Rockwell took off his glasses and smoothed out a few wrinkles on his face, but he kept his pipe firmly in his mouth. In his idealized vision of himself, where he shows us the face he wants the world to see, he is clearly a proud pipe smoker.

I became a full-fledged pipe smoker in 1978, but I was dabbling with a pipe a couple of years before that, trying to give up cigarettes. But at the time I was experimenting, in 1976, the president of the United States, Gerald Ford, was rarely pictured without his pipe. The fact that he lived to be 93, longer than any other president in history, says a great deal about the relaxing benefits of moderate pipe smoking.

But throughout the 1980s, '90s and to today, the message has been that all smoking is bad. The commercials started by saying it is unhealthy and ended by portraying it as pure evil. The rationale for this propaganda blitz was the very real damage caused by heavy cigarette smoking, but moderate cigar and pipe smoking were bundled with cigarettes as if they were all the same.

The result is that all things tobacco have been condemned. Smokers have been ostracized. They have been demonized. They are today's lepers. It is difficult in most places to smoke at work, or in a restaurant, or even in a bar. Smoking on an airplane ... are you crazy? There are laws banning smoking in cars in certain situations.

As someone who travels frequently, I have to make special efforts to find a smoking room in a hotel. Spending a day at the ballpark means spending a day without my pipe. A growing number of cities are banning smoking outside in so-called "public areas." We have seen judges award custody of children to the non-smoking parent only because they don't smoke.

I bought my first pack of cigarettes when I was 12, no questions asked. At age 57, I was "carded" by a teenager at Walgreens when I bought some pipe tobacco. Of course, it is insane to allow a 12-year-old boy to buy tobacco products without even asking for proof of identification, showing that he is at least 18 years old. The only thing more insane is to ask a man three years shy of his 60th birthday for proof of identification showing that he is at least 18 years old.

Our new prohibition is masked in many different forms, but the key is to declare property rights obsolete and to mock anyone who disagrees as being old-fashioned. Just change the meaning of words.

In the best tradition of Orwell's "1984," private buildings have been reclassified as "public" buildings if they are open to the public. For hundreds of years, the difference between a private building and a public building depended upon who owned it -- not who visited it.

Historically, the public building was City Hall, the DMV or the local police station, while the private building was the town's bank, commercial office building or popular restaurant.

But today, by modern definitions, there is no such thing as a private building. They are all public buildings, and if you cherish property rights, you should be very worried. By changing this definition, the prohibitionists are able to trample over the property rights of individuals as a way to ban smoking.

Not long ago, The New York Times ran an editorial advocating a ban on all indoor smoking -- yes, no exceptions, all indoor smoking -- while several California cities have passed laws banning most outdoor smoking.

These are similar to fascist proposals and prohibitions. No, let me rephrase that: These ARE fascist proposals and prohibitions. They fit nicely with our new sense of conformity as a society, where we increasingly live and work on top of one another and forfeit our privacy and individuality. Nearly all airports have intolerably long security lines, and invasive body searches are not unusual. As we submit physically to all this inhuman herding, it is only natural to succumb psychologically to the herd mentality. Our cities are crammed with identical-looking office buildings with hermetically sealed windows and crowded elevators. Even the suburbs have become congested.

Supermarkets smell like office buildings, which smell like hospitals, which smell like airports. Chrome and disinfectant are the order of the day. There is little tolerance for the old-fashioned aromas of cigar and pipe tobaccos, and little patience for the slow, time-honored traditions of carefully packing a pipe, puffing and tamping, fiddling and relighting, and all those other activities associated with relaxed pipe smoking.

We live in a world that glorifies all things new, fast-paced, sanitized and sterilized ... in a society that claims to value diversity and tolerance, but when it comes to tobacco, forget about it.

Despite the barrage of propaganda, there are a handful of us who persist, who continue to enjoy our pipes, who have discovered the exciting world of pipe collecting. More and more young people are becoming interested in the hobby, and a surprising number of them are becoming very good pipe makers who are attracted to the infinite possibilities for creating artwork that is functional.

I attended the World Pipe Smoking Contest in St. Petersburg last October. It was my first time in Russia, and St. Petersburg is a magnificent city. But what struck me most was the large number of pipe enthusiasts in their 20s and 30s. They were from Russia, Italy, Spain, Sweden, the Ukraine and dozens of other countries.

You find the same at the Chicago Pipe Show each May, where the universal language among more than a thousand participants is pipes -- pipe collecting, pipe making, pipe trading and pipe smoking. Even if the intolerant ones were to ban smoking during the show, we still would find a way to enjoy our pipes together. (Editor's note: Illinois politicians predictably banned smoking at the Chicago Pipe Show within a year of this writing, but the show organizers now rent a circus-sized tent where everyone congregates and enjoys their pipes.)

So the question is: What is the allure of pipe collecting and pipe smoking when we are assaulted daily with the message that unless we quit smoking, we are not wanted? We can go to dinner parties and to weddings and picnics and to all kinds of social events, just as long as we don't smoke.

There might be many reasons why you picked up a pipe in the first place -- maybe your father or grandfather smoked a pipe, or maybe you've always liked the image of the pipe smoker for a variety of reasons -- it doesn't really matter.

What is important to understand is that everyone who smokes a pipe in the 21st century is a rebel. You are not a sheep that goes along with the flock, you are an individualist who refuses to be bullied by the mob.

Pipe smoking today is considered such an extremely anti-social activity that we have become social outlaws, and we're willing to live with that.

Would we also be willing to become political outlaws? If pipe smoking were banned by government decree, would we continue to smoke our pipes? I know I would, and I suspect most of you would, too.

Yes, we are all quiet revolutionaries.

Our goal, however, is not to topple governments. It is to be left alone by those governments so we can enjoy our pipes together in peace. This is not a minor matter for most of us. In fact, the freedom to enjoy our pipes is a condition for our happiness. As Mark Twain once said, "If I cannot smoke in heaven, then I shall not go."

But it is not enough to be a pipe smoker merely to be defiant. We are pipe smokers, and pipe collectors, because we have discovered a world of fulfillment that is unknown to more than 99 percent of the world's population.

We have discovered the Zen-like relaxation and meditation that pipe smoking brings.

We have discovered the tactile pleasures involved with holding a pipe, along with the wonderful soothing of all our senses, which pipe smoking gently provides.

Many people have called pipes sensual -- and for good reason.

We have discovered the intense excitement that we feel when buying a new pipe that we really want -- a feeling like no other.

At some point, we have come to realize that our pipe collections are invaluable to us, much more so than any jewelry collection.

I mention jewelry because of an incident that occurred last summer, when I was at a small dinner party in Sacramento hosted by California Governor Arnold Schwarzenegger. I was seated next to Gail Gardner, whose husband, Bob, is a famous Los Angeles photographer and one of Arnold's longtime photographers. I have known Bob and Gail for many years, and I casually mentioned to Gail that I was interested in hiring Bob to take pictures of some of my pipes. Gail looked surprised after she realized I was referring to smoking pipes.

"You don't still smoke a pipe, do you?" she asked.

"I do," I replied. "I try to enjoy two bowls a day, and if it's a good day, three bowls."

A few weeks later we were all three in Bob's photo studio, where I spread out dozens of pipes. Bob is the ultimate perfectionist, and it took three hours and twenty minutes (I was looking at the clock every five minutes!) before he took his first photo. He kept changing the lighting, the background, the position of the pipes -- you name it -- until he felt it was just right.

His patience paid off. Ulf Noltensmeier, an Old World craftsman who makes the S. Bang pipes along with Per Hansen, said Bob captured the "soul" of the pipes. Before Ulf saw them, however, Gail had spent countless hours in Photoshop trying to make each pipe look as crisp, sharp and shiny as possible. The more she studied the individual pipes in the photographs, the more she appreciated them as the works of art they are.

"They are like little jewels," she said. "I had no idea pipes could be so beautiful."

That is an important reason why we are pipe collectors -- because we appreciate the beauty of our pipes. It makes no difference if they are hand made or factory made. What counts is what we perceive to be their aesthetic beauty and rarity.

But these characteristics are only on the outside. It is the inside that counts most, where a well-lit pipe with our favorite tobacco kept barely smoldering with occasional puffs -- that is heaven for us.

For me, most of my smoking is a solitary activity, which is especially good for relaxation and meditation. I usually smoke two bowls in the evening, when I read, write, or watch a mystery on TV that I have TiVoed. My favorite shows include Columbo, Perry Mason, Sherlock Holmes, Maigret, Miss Marple, Poirot and, most recently, Monk.

My mind is only half-watching as I drift into a state of total calm. I have one of those blood pressure monitors that I bought from the drug store, and at some point I try to remember to take my blood pressure. Once my pipe is barely smoldering, I take my blood pressure, and invariably it drops to the exact extent to which the pipe is helping me relax.

After a long day without smoking -- a day filled with work, working out, interacting with many people at the office, and family dinner -- then there is my time ... an aged tobacco that is mellow like an aged wine, and filling it into a pipe made by a friend or someone I know about and admire, or by a factory that built its reputation on a commitment to excellence, and settling back and savoring the experience.

Each pipe I smoke has its own story, and these stories represent a part of my life, a part of who I am. I always remember when I acquired a pipe, and that memory takes me back to a different time and place. It is a part of my past, enjoyed in the present, and available for the future -- for many years to come.

Nothing helps me relax like smoking a pipe. Not yoga, or petting the dog or cat, or alcohol, or hypnosis. I've tried them all, and nothing compares to relaxing with a pipe. The fact that some men over the centuries have known this only reinforces my conviction that I am on the right track.

But pipe smoking is not always a solitary activity. There are still a few terrific pipe stores in business, and I try to visit many whenever I travel to new cities. When I am at home, on Saturdays I frequently stop by the original Tinder

Box in Santa Monica for a pipe, a cup of coffee, and good conversation with fellow pipe smokers. We usually swap tobaccos as well as stories, and we always have fun.

It is the social aspects of pipe smoking that have made pipe shows so popular around the world. In the old days, there was no need for a pipe show because you could smoke your pipe pretty much anywhere you wanted. But as we have become ostracized and isolated, there is a need for us to get together with our pipes and tobaccos, whether it is a banquet dinner in Seattle or a pipe show in Chicago, New York or even St. Petersburg, Russia.

Pipe shows are just so much fun. They open up a world unlike any that exists today. It is a world of friendship and camaraderie, of buying and selling, of trading and swapping, of meeting and mingling with pipe experts who span the globe -- and we're all experts when it comes to our own pipe collections. It is a world of smoking without the slightest bit of self-consciousness, at least for a few hours, a world where people might have almost nothing in common except for their shared passion for pipes and tobaccos. And that passion is a common bond that breaks down language barriers and overrides all else.

Another development that keeps us enthusiastic is the Internet. We can look at hundreds if not thousands of new and used pipes for sale from all over the world. We can log on to one of the forums and make new friends with this common interest.

And what about the wide variety of choices within this field? Whether it is the type of pipes or what makes a good smoker, there are as many opinions as there are pipe smokers.

It does not matter what your specific interests are. What counts is to know that for you, when it comes to your pipes, you are king. You are always right, and that applies even if you change your mind!

I remember once at a Los Angeles Pipe Show when Vernon Vig received an award for "Outstanding Contribution to the Hobby." Vernon was selected because of his work uniting pipe clubs in the United States with pipe clubs from around the world. But Vernon would have none of it. He said his real contribution to the hobby was in buying and selling as an ordinary collector.

"Over the past 50 years," he said, "I've purchased many fine pipes at high prices -- which has been good for pipe makers and pipe shops. Now I'm reselling many of those same pipes at low prices -- which is good for pipe smokers."

I love Vernon's attitude toward pipe collecting -- he does it for fun and for no other reason.

The fact is, there is room for people of all income brackets when it comes to pipe collecting. A seven dollar CustomBilt pipe from 10 years ago might sell for $20 today and several hundred dollars in 40 years -- because CustomBilt stopped making pipes years ago and the ones still available will become increasingly rare.

This is even truer for high-grade Dunhills, Charatans and other English pipes, and it applies to the beautiful pipes from Denmark, Italy, America, Japan, Germany, Russia, Ireland and many other countries. Once the pipe maker dies, those pipes are increasingly scarce. If there is a demand, the price will rise. A $40 Sixten Ivarsson pipe sold in 1964 at the old Pipe Dan store in Copenhagen could easily fetch $2,000 on eBay today.

My own prediction for the future is that pipe collecting will be even more popular and specialized with an emphasis on hand-made pipes and rare factory pipes. Good grain, beautiful shapes, good smoking qualities and the difficulty in obtaining the pipe will determine its value, and I expect the prices to continue rising. But who knows?

In 40 years, that $2,000 Sixten Ivarsson pipe might sell for $20,000 ... or it might sell for $20. We have no way of knowing for sure. If the prices go up, that will be good for my heirs -- they'll get rich! If prices go down, that is good for me -- I'll be able to buy more pipes and add freely to my collection.

I don't buy pipes in order to make money. In fact, my

wife says I make money in order to buy pipes.

Relaxing with a pipe is a lost art today, yet something this much fun, with such a storied past and so many rewards, won't stay lost forever.

All of us in the hobby have discovered the unlimited number of pleasures derived from pipe smoking and pipe collecting, and we are the lucky ones. It is as if we have uncovered a secret treasure that is centuries old.

The first pipe club in the world was founded in Germany in 1876, and it still exists today. A group of pipe enthusiasts in the city of Wurselen decided to get together for occasional parties and conversations about their favorite pipes and tobaccos. There was only one time period when the club was banned -- the 12 years from 1933-1945 when Adolf Hitler and the Nazis were in charge. That's an interesting fact to keep in mind if you feel intimidated by today's self-righteous and militant anti-smoking movement.

At the St. Petersburg show, I was surprised to learn that Peter the Great was an enthusiastic pipe smoker 300 years ago. This is the man who brought European culture to Russia.

That culture included the music of German composer Johann Sebastian Bach, who famously compared his lifespan to that of his pipe in a poem he wrote for his wife. Bach turned to his pipe for relaxation, contemplation and what he called "fruitful meditation." He ended the poem with these words:

> And so, puffing contentedly,
> On land, at sea, at home, abroad,
> I smoke my pipe and worship God.

As I looked around the luxurious ballroom at the Gala Dinner of the St. Petersburg Pipe Show, I thought about the fact that great men throughout history have turned to their pipes for comfort and solace. My mood that night was enthusiastically upbeat because of the excitement of the crowd, with good music and entertainment, good food, good wine, good friends, good dancing and good pipes!

I was watching so many pipe enthusiasts from all over the world, young and old, who were having such a great time, and I savored the moment. I was looking at a room full of independent thinking people who refuse to be bent into submission by the tyranny of the majority. It occurred to me that something this special, this much fun, that has such a rich history as well as a strong contemporary appeal to so many individualists worldwide, must continue to prosper.

Most people are under a great deal of stress these days, and many of them aren't having a whole lot of fun in their lives, which is why I believe it is only a matter of time before they discover the fun that we're having as pipe collectors and the relaxing, stress-reducing benefits of moderate pipe smoking. We are indeed leading a quiet revolution.

CHAPTER TWO

~~~~~

PIPE THOUGHTS WHILE TRAVELING IN EUROPE

The judges in Wurselen, Germany getting ready for an international pipe smoking contest with hundreds of participants representing dozens of countries from around the world. The contestants take these contests very seriously.

This chapter offers my reflections on pipes in the fall of 2008 when my wife Carole and I were traveling through Europe, on both business and vacation, and even with time for a few pipe days in Germany, Denmark and Ireland. I remember that the world economy looked to be at risk, with stock markets crashing daily by huge percentages in China, Europe, the United States and every place there was one. When the world is collapsing around you, there is nothing so soothing as one's pipes and pipe reflections.

* * * * *

It is my fervent hope that 200 years from now, pipe smokers will be reading these words. I say this not with any illusions of literary grandeur but because of the unique and enduring nature of the subject matter -- pipes.

Pipe smoking has been practiced in a variety of forms for hundreds of years, but it is being threatened by the worldwide campaign to wipe out all smoking. This makes it even more remarkable that in recent years there has developed a whole world of pipe enthusiasts who can be found in forums on the Internet, at pipe shows and pipe club meetings, searching and bidding on eBay, and in many cases taking up pipe making either as a hobby or as a career. I find it fascinating that pipes continue to attract young people -- not with the same numbers as in the past, but with an intensity and knowledge never seen before.

Pipes are very different from cigars and cigarettes. They have a much more interesting history than either one. They are also different in that their users frequently enjoy them for a lifetime and actually have a "relationship," for want of a better word, with their pipes.

We collect pipes, clean and polish them, and display them on racks or in cabinets. We get to know them, and learn the peculiarities of each one. We associate events and people with them, and they provide a wonderful way to remember things past. Each pipe that I own is a unique source of pleasant memories.

Over the years, the materials for pipes have changed, beginning with Indians smoking stone pipes many centuries ago. In the 1500s the clay tobacco pipe was introduced, and since then we have seen smokers attracted to meerschaum, porcelain, corncob and other materials for pipes. But it is the briar pipe, beginning in the 19th century, that swept the pipe-smoking world.

The images of the pipe smoker have changed over the years, from public smoking everywhere to private pipe collecting at home. There has been a dramatic shift from quantity to quality, from a dozen pipe bowls a day to a dozen a month, from mass produced pipes and tobacco to handmade artisan pipes with specially blended and aged tobaccos, from millions of pipe smokers who took it all for granted, to thousands of pipe smokers who are secretly passionate about their pipe collecting. They search the Internet for rare finds and eagerly attend pipe shows so they can meet their favorite pipe makers and share their experiences with like-minded individuals from all over the world.

These were a few of my thoughts as I attended the European Championship in Pipe Smoking contest in Wurselen, Germany on the weekend of Oct. 4 - 5, 2008. There were five of us representing the United States. Unfortunately, this was the same weekend as the CORPS pipe show in Richmond, Virginia. I debated whether to attend the pipe show in America or to attend the international show representing America, and decided on the latter. I only wish I could have attended both ... and done a better job representing my country.

The contest itself was quite remarkable, with hundreds of people from around the world competing to see who could keep his pipe lit the longest after using only two matches in the first few minutes. The winner was an Italian who kept his bowl smoldering for more than three-and-a-half hours! For me, it was intended to be fun, not competition, but I was clearly in the minority. You would not believe how seriously some people take this contest. It reminded me of sitting in an auditorium many decades ago taking the SAT college entrance exams.

Jotham Tausig of Ann Arbor, Michigan, champion at the 2008 Chicago Pipe Show contest, was our leader with a time of more than one hour. Jotham told me that he had the same impression about the seriousness with which this contest was being taken. "I could see one man's hands trembling as the officials announced the rules and instructions for the contest," he said.

At one point during the contest, I started tamping my pipe and the woman competing next to me (yes, woman), with a thick accent, said, "No!" and I realized my mistake: All tamping must be done with the pipe in your mouth, not in your hand. "Sorry," I said. "I forgot."

Despite smoking a pipe for many years, I do not claim to be a master of being able to keep my pipe lit for so long, and my non-competitive time of 47 minutes supported that contention.

The contest was sponsored by the International Committee of Pipe Clubs, and the theme of the show was, "Relax with your pipe," which is a sentiment I wholeheartedly endorse. I save my competitive juices for the business world, and I seek relaxation -- not competition -- from my pipe. Still, it could be that I am just making excuses.

There was also a pipe show on Saturday and Sunday in the hall outside the big room where the competition took place. It was sponsored by Peter Heinrichs, who owns several well-stocked and successful pipe stores in and around Cologne, Germany. The pipe show and competition were held in the most unlikely place -- a high school. Attending and welcoming us were the Mayor of Wurselen, several members of the German Parliament and a 95-year-old woman who loves her pipe and does not look a day over 65.

Several legendary pipe makers were there, including Poul Winslow, Tom Eltang, Kurt Balleby, Luigi Viprati, Karl Heinz Joura and Wolfgang Becker. In addition, many

30-something artisan pipe makers from Germany were there, including the very talented Reiner Thilo, Juergen Moritz, Frank Axmacher and Uwe Jopp. There were many others whose names I don't know, but who are obviously talented pipe makers.

I was hoping to meet Oliver Brandt and his son, Max, both of whom make pipes, but unfortunately they were not there. I picked up one of their pipes recently and am very pleased with it. The straight grain is gorgeous, the pipe is light in weight, it has a comfortable feel to it and is a pleasure to smoke.

At this show, I bought a special Balleby bulldog and my first Cornelius Maenz pipe. Cornelius was not there, but Per Bilhall was selling a handful of Maenz pipes. The one I bought is a small bent pipe with a deceptively large bowl capacity, and I was extremely pleased with it right off the bat. His mouthpieces are amazingly comfortable, and a pipe cleaner is easily pushed through the mouthpiece to the bottom of the bowl.

I did notice one disturbing trend from several of the newer German pipe makers, and I wish they would abandon the practice: I am talking about using a curved drill bit for bent pipes. I know that some French and Italian pipe makers have used these drill bits over the years, but as a consumer, I have never been happy with them.

For one thing, there is no way for a bent pipe drilled that way to pass the "pipe cleaner test." For another, if I want to open the air hole inside the shank a little, I cannot do it. A straight drill bit will not fit into a U-shaped curve. If a slight cake builds up inside the shank, I can't remove it. If I want to run a tube brush with alcohol through the shank to clean it, I can't do that either.

In fact, I saw one beautifully shaped bowl by one of the young German pipe makers, and I was tempted to buy it. But when it failed to pass the pipe cleaner test, I asked if he had used a curved drill bit, and he smiled excitedly and said yes, taking pride in having mastered something difficult. His English and my German were both bad, so Einar Fjeldvig, one of Poul Ilsted's most enthusiastic collectors from Denmark, and a very friendly fellow, managed to translate for both of us. With Einar's help, I said I would like to buy a similar pipe but only if it were drilled with a straight drill bit.

I was supposed to be selling copies of the German edition of my book, but that was difficult because of the language issue. Most of the German collectors said they already had it, and the others who looked at it wanted it in French, Spanish, Dutch, Italian or Russian. But the good news about having the German edition of the book was that on Page 99, there is a Lars Ivarsson pipe pictured that was very similar in design to the pipe with the curved drill bit opening. (This is on Page 79 of the American edition: the pipe in the lower right corner.) I explained, through Einar, that Lars used a straight drill bit and that his pipe easily passed the pipe cleaner test. The pipe maker seemed genuinely curious and appreciative of our conversation, though for all I know he cursed and swore about what a jerk I was after I walked away.

I do worry sometimes about being so particular about what I like. Most pipe makers tell me they appreciate customers who know what they want, but I sometimes wonder after I go through my list if they don't say, "What a pain in the neck that guy is!"

To avoid confusion, I should clarify in stating that the curved airway that I am describing has nothing to do with the shape of the tobacco chamber. Some tobacco chambers are U-shaped and others V-shaped. Some people prefer a V-shaped drilling, but I always want a U-shaped bottom inside the tobacco chamber, even if the pipe appears to be conical or otherwise outwardly tends toward a V-shape.

I use the "three white square rule," which I discovered by accident. The white squares come from Vauen's pipe cleaners, which have blue-and-white (or red-and-white) swirls. When I put one of those cleaners inside my pipe, I like to see a minimum of three white squares inside the bowl. Nearly all of my best smoking pipes pass this test. Try it on your own pipes and see if this doesn't make sense to you. I am not sure why U-shaped chambers smoke better for me, or why I have trouble smoking pipes with V-shaped chambers, but I am interested if anyone has a theory.

It has been many years since I collected old Charatans, Barlings and Dunhills, and today I probably would not have alterations made on those pipes because they are collectibles. Rich Esserman and Bob Palermo make a compelling case that they should be preserved in as close to their original state as possible. It is easy for me to agree, however, since I rarely collect those pipes anymore, and the ones in my collection were modified years ago.

Nearly all the pipes I buy today are handmade by a pipe maker I know and respect, and they never have a problem following my specifications. For example, if I buy a J. Alan pipe from Jeff Gracik -- a brilliant young American pipe maker -- he knows to open the draft hole inside the shank a little wider than usual; to open the mouthpiece so an extra fluffy cleaner goes through the tenon end and out the lip end with virtually no resistance; to sand down the mouthpiece at the lip end so that it is between 3.6 mm and 3.9 mm in thickness from top to bottom, and to pass the "three white square" test at the bottom of the tobacco chamber. One of the reasons Jeff finds these guidelines easy to follow for my pipes is because they are very close to his own guidelines for all of his pipes.

My advice to all pipe collectors is to experiment with various openings of the draft hole, thicknesses of the mouthpiece and diameters for the bottom of the tobacco chamber, and keep notes on what you like best. Then, when you see a pipe that you are drawn to because of the way it looks, go ahead and buy it (if it is in your price range). If it does not smoke as well as you expected, contact the pipe maker and offer to pay a little extra to have your modifications made. Most pipe makers will be happy to oblige, and they will usually do so without charging extra. If it then smokes the way you want, ask the pipe maker to keep your specifications and tell him you'll be back for more.

Trust me, he won't resent it!

If it is a new factory pipe or one made by an overseas pipe maker, you can either mail it to them with a letter of explanation, or you can pay a local pipe repairman or pipe maker to custom tailor the pipe for you. I've done this many times and have never regretted it.

Einar Fjeldvig and I agreed that a comfortable mouthpiece makes all the difference. "I could have a beautiful pipe, but if it has a thick mouthpiece that is uncomfortable, I don't want to smoke it," he said. "In fact, I would rather smoke an inferior pipe with a comfortable mouthpiece than the most beautiful pipe in the world if it is uncomfortable." My sentiments exactly -- which is why I am so adamant about having my pipes customized for my comfort.

What struck me most at the show was the beauty of so many handmade pipes and the commitment and enthusiasm of the young European pipe makers. I had the same impression last May at the Chicago Pipe Show while looking at the work of so many talented new pipe makers from America. This bodes well for the future of the hobby.

One of the attractions of pipe collecting is that there is room for everyone. There are collectors who specialize in new Castellos or old Charatans or any one of a hundred other brands. Some look for Radice's or Ashton's or Ferndown's newest pipes, while others look for rare older pipes. There is no question that many of the name-brand English pipes had some truly outstanding pipe makers going back more than a century, such as Horry Jameson at Comoy and GBD.

I remember when Bo Nordh once told me that when an expert pipe maker dies, we are all the worse for it. "Picture someone who has been making pipes at Dunhill for 40 or 50 years, and then he dies," Bo said. "All his knowledge goes with him."

While I agreed with Bo at the time, in hindsight I realize that what he said is only partly true. We can appreciate, and learn from, their expertise whenever we study one of these increasingly rare pipes. It is the reason Jess Chonowitsch has spent much time studying Dunhill shapes from catalogs produced in the 1920s.

Two days after attending the international pipe show in Germany, Carole and I flew to Copenhagen, and I couldn't help but reminisce. The airport seemed so busy, modern and international, so unlike my first impression of it from the summer of 1980. At that time, my brother was getting married in Norway, and my connecting flight stopped at the Copenhagen airport. My one-hour layover lasted a full eight hours because of an air traffic controllers' work slowdown.

Here are two "ifs" that have haunted me many times since then: if I had known I had eight hours before my flight would leave, I could have gone into downtown Copenhagen; and if I had known how to find Sixten Ivarsson and his workshop, I could have spent the day there!

As it turned out, there was a pipe shop at the airport (impossible to imagine today), and I spent several hours studying the pipes. At that time, I had not smoked an Ivarsson pipe, but I selected a bent sandblast that clearly was a Sixten shape.

The next time I visited Copenhagen was in 1995, and I have written extensively about how impressed I was by the pipes made by Jess Chonowitsch, S. Bang and Lars and Nanna Ivarsson.

This trip was different because I did not see Jess, Lars or Nanna. She gave birth to a baby boy on the opening day of the pipe show, and Lars was helping out as a proud grandpa. That's the good news.

The bad news, the incredibly sad and tragic news, is that Bonnie Chonowitsch is suffering from ALS, known in America as "Lou Gehrig's Disease." Jess and Bonnie are the closest couple I have ever known. They have stayed at our house and we have stayed at theirs; we have spent many days together, and I cannot ever once remember them arguing. They met as teenagers, fell in love, raised two beautiful daughters, and lived happily as a warm and loving family. Thank God the daughters, and their children, live nearby and give Jess and Bonnie love and support during this unimaginably painful time.

Carole told me that when she walked through King's Park in Copenhagen, "all I could think about was Bonnie." That's because the last time we were there, two years ago, Carole, Bonnie and Annette Ivarsson, Lars' wife, walked through that park after lunch while Jess, Lars and I smoked a pipe bowl at the tobacconist My Own Blend in downtown Copenhagen.

I thought back to my first meeting with Jess, and I remember being impressed that his knowledge of pipe making was so vast. When he showed me his pipes after lunch, I knew his skill was at the highest possible level.

At that lunch, I pulled out a beautiful billiard-shaped pipe to show Jess, and he asked if he could hold it. Quickly, using the cover of a matchbook that was sitting on the table, he sliced it between the·wood of the shank and the vulcanite mouthpiece. He did not wiggle it in, nor did he try to force it through what was a very tiny gap. In fact, I had not even noticed that there was a slight open space between the wood and the mouthpiece. So when he did this effortlessly, on his first try, I sat there open-mouthed. His manual dexterity, and jeweler's eye, were demonstrated in a split second. I really had never seen anything like it.

Jess stopped making pipes as Bonnie's symptoms started to worsen.

"She was there for me every step of the way when I was making pipes," he said. "She came to the shows, she was always supportive, and I want to be there for her at this time."

On this trip, Carole had gone to Mass to pray for Bonnie and Jess, and we talked at length about her youthfulness, her energy and her love of life. "When I think of Bonnie, I always think of her smiling," Carole said, speaking for both of us. (Editor's note: Bonnie died on February 22, 2012.)

Earlier that day, I met with the S. Bang pipe makers,

Ulf Noltensmeier and Per Hansen. Over the years, I have visited their workshop many times, and I remember when they moved from the one they had been in for more than 20 years to the one they are in now because of the effects of globalization.

I watched as the original location changed from a building with friendly neighbors and small businesses to impersonal, high tech companies featuring rows of computers, phone banks and big screen television monitors. Young executives on their cell phones, wearing expensive shirts and ties and even more expensive shoes, would step outside occasionally for a cigarette break. Suddenly an Old World pipe making workshop had become out of place in its own home.

But Ulf and Per had no problem resettling, and they have continued to make beautiful pipes. We talked about the W.O. Larsen store, which was closed four years ago. They told me that Svend Bang worked for Ole Larsen's father and briefly with Ole before starting his own pipe and tobacco store in 1968. He hired Ulf and Per a few years later with the idea of having a large pipe workshop that would compete with Larsen pipes. But Ulf and Per told Mr. Bang that they did not want to oversee the production of thousands of pipes. They wanted to make a small number of high grade pipes instead.

"So Svend Bang envisioned doing what W.O. Larsen was doing, while you wanted to do what Sixten Ivarsson was doing -- is that about it?" I asked.

"That's exactly it." Per said.

Ulf said one of the most common questions they are asked is if anyone will ever succeed them.

"I am very encouraged to hear you say there are so many promising new pipe makers," he said. "That could be really good news for the future of pipe smoking."

After we said goodbye, I visited the recently moved My Own Blend pipe and cigar store, now located only a few blocks from where the W.O. Larsen Store was. My Own Blend and Davidoff have teamed up to create a wonderful store just off the "walking street" in downtown Copenhagen. They have a terrific selection of pipes and tobaccos, and their specialty is blending your tobaccos however you want, just like Alfred Dunhill used to do in London.

I was happy to see Lasse Berg, who really knows pipes and tobaccos. Lasse had left the business for a few years, so I was surprised and delighted to see him when we walked through the door. He always does such a great job recreating the original Rattray's No. 7 Reserve -- it is one of my favorites.

But this time I wanted something similar but with a slight variation. I told Lasse that I'd like it if he could use something like Condor for part of the Virginias, and he said yes, he had some dark Virginia that had been treated with essence of rose oil. This leaves that mild soapy aftertaste.

For many years I resisted all offers of Condor precisely because of that soapy, or perfume-like, aftertaste. I found it hard to believe when Jim Benjamin told me that Condor was the most popular pipe tobacco blend in the world at one time.

Whenever I bought an estate pipe that had a hint of perfume or a soapy taste near the bottom of the bowl, I would freak out. A few times I separated the mouthpiece from the bowl and then put both inside a jar filled with denatured alcohol solvent. I put a lid on the jar and let them soak for 24 hours. I would then take them out and use tube brushes dipped in alcohol to continue cleaning them. Of course, these pipes would then need to be restained, polished and buffed, but at least the soapy taste would evaporate. I have read of many other techniques for getting rid of the aromas of perfume or soap in the bowl, but this is the technique I use. It is radical, and I am not recommending it for everyone, but I mention it because it works for me.

So why would I want Lasse to make his version of No. 7 Reserve with a slight soapy aftertaste? The answer is variety. I have certain blends that I like best, but every so often I like to try something new for a change of pace.

In 1996 I visited Sturk's Tobacconists in

Cape Town, South Africa and bought eight ounces of their English/Oriental bulk blend, Balkan Special. I put that bag in a picnic cooler and did not retrieve it until 12 years later. When I smoked my first bowl of the tobacco, it left a very slight soapy aftertaste, and it was wonderful! But this is only for a change of pace -- maybe one bowl per month, and I smoke between two and three bowls a day.

The main point about seeing Lasse Berg is that it was so comforting to find a real tobacconist with a passion for pipes. He is extremely knowledgeable and friendly. Along the same lines, I was happy to see Dr. Uli Woehrle at the pipe show in Wurselen. Uli is a retired pediatrician who has been an enthusiastic pipe collector for many decades. He fits the European definition of the old-fashioned "true collector" because he only collects pipes and never sells them.

In the 1946 Sherlock Holmes movie "Dressed to Kill," starring Basil Rathbone and Nigel Bruce, there is a revealing scene in which an older man is flirting with a beautiful young woman who wants one of his musical boxes. She asks him for it, and he replies, "You put me in an awkward position. I'm a collector, you know, and a collector buys but never sells."

She presses, "If the price were high enough?"

And he says, "Price has nothing to do with it. It's the principle of the thing."

That is an interesting image of a "true collector," and we can understand the sentiment of wanting to hang on to one's valuable collection, but most of us believe pipe collecting would be pretty dull if no one ever traded a pipe. Uli is a very special person in the hobby, and I always learn from him. I have long admired him for his discriminating taste in high grades, but I was even more impressed by the way he offered encouragement and praise to some of the younger pipe makers at the Wurselen show.

After saying goodbye to the new, modern and busy Copenhagen, Carole and I flew to Dublin, equally modern and busy, where we stayed for several days. Carole wanted to see the Book of Kells at Trinity College, and luckily for me, the Peterson pipe store is located right across the street. I spent about an hour studying the beautiful pipes before finally deciding on one -- a "Baskerville" shape from the Sherlock Holmes series.

Almost next door to the Peterson store is Fox's Cigars, which sells a great English blend of pipe tobacco called Bankers. I bought a small amount of the bulk version because the aroma of that tobacco in a giant tin, which held about two pounds, was simply magnificent.

After our tour of the Trinity College Library, I headed back to our hotel, where we had reserved a smoking room. I opened the window -- and it opened so wide that the room had an indoor/outdoor feel to it -- and smoked this wonderful Peterson pipe, filled with the very delicious Bankers tobacco, and contemplated the joy of pipe smoking. I spent time studying the beautiful shape of the Peterson pipe and marveled at how well it smoked.

I have written a great deal about how much I like handmade artisan pipes, and of how my appreciation of their pipes is enhanced if I know and like the pipe maker.

But this does not mean that I only like handmade pipes. Some of my favorite pipes over the years were made in the factories of famous pipe companies such as Peterson.

The bowl was turned beautifully, the silver work is magnificent, and the bent P-lip mouthpiece is comfortable as a change of pace. Whenever I pick up this pipe and study its shape, color and grain, I am reminded that there is a tradition of more than a hundred years of excellence in pipe making behind it.

During our trip to Europe, Carole and I visited several art museums in different cities, including Brussels and Frankfurt. At the one in Copenhagen, we saw many beautiful paintings and sculptures. There were scenes of beauty, heroism, hardship, struggle, victory and other settings that left us feeling excited and inspired. These paintings were in the classical section. In the contemporary section, with modern art, we saw paintings that looked like an artist's nightmare, in addition to the familiar canvasses that looked like children created the paintings using their fingers, or like the floor of a room that was being painted, where the painters dripped paint and then stepped in it.

After leaving that museum, I read a newspaper story about a ban on smoking at Pennsylvania state colleges and universities, not just inside but outside as well. If you were a student at one of these schools, you could not smoke in a classroom or a dorm, nor would there be any designated smoking room. But outside? Yes, no smoking outside anywhere on campus. That clearly is prohibition, and there is something perverse about the notion of no smoking anywhere outdoors. No wonder someone made a T-shirt with the slogan, "Smoking is healthier than fascism."

I was struck by the contrast, however, between the beautiful artwork from 100 years ago, when pipe smoking was a respected pastime, and the nihilistic artwork from today, where intolerance of smoking and prohibition are the orders of the day. Is there a connection? I don't know, but it certainly felt that way. Perhaps it has something to do with the fact that one was ugly, chaotic and angry while the other appeared beautiful, embracing and inspiring.

At a Dublin art museum I saw a colorful painting of the Connaught Brigade of 1798 that featured five soldiers, two of whom were happy pipe smokers. It occurred to me that smoking started centuries ago with pipes, not cigarettes, and will continue for centuries to come with pipes and not cigarettes. The latter is the source of the hostility toward smoking that is so prevalent today.

The fact that pipes have a tradition that dates back hundreds of years puts history squarely on our side. When scolding bureaucrats criticize your pipe smoking, they are not only attacking you, they are attacking Johann Sebastian Bach, C.S. Lewis, J.R.R. Tolkein, Sir Arthur Conan Doyle, Mark Twain, Georges Simenon, Claude Monet, Vicent Van Gogh, Auguste Rodin, Albert Einstein, Bertrand Russell, Jean Paul Sartre, General Douglas MacArthur, financier J.P. Morgan, American President Andrew Jackson, Egyptian President Anwar Sadat, Russian Czar Peter the Great and hundreds of other giants of history who found contemplation and relaxation with their pipes.

Relaxation is a lost art today. Just look at the wild gyrations of the stock market in October 2008, which occurred during our trip to Europe. I recently heard someone use the phrase "nightmare pill," and I can't help but think that is what so many people have taken.

But as the masses go marching toward a new world order of no smoking and no exceptions, while paying lip service to "diversity and tolerance," we pipe smokers are finding our own little world away from the crowds. I always find it reassuring to read pipe journals and blogs and to attend pipe shows in America and around the world -- to know there are others who think like me. That is why I wanted to share some of my recent travel experiences and pipe reflections with you.

Let's hope our pipe smoking successors in future generations will be able to find the same fun, camaraderie and pleasure that we pipe smokers are enjoying in the 21st century, just as our ancestors dating back hundreds of years did. They might have experienced pipe smoking in different ways from us, but no doubt they were equally satisfying ways.

Pipe smoking and pipe collecting will continue to evolve, but I sincerely doubt they will ever be extinguished. They have too rich a history, and they're just too much fun.

CHAPTER THREE

2009 CHICAGO PIPE SHOW

Frank Burla (left) founded what is known as the Chicago Pipe Show and ran it for 15 years before being succeeded by his friend and colleague, Craig Cobine.

While this is a report on the 2009 Chicago Pipe Show, it really is a brief history of the Chicago show and could apply to any year. My goal was to capture the feelings that make this show so special for so many people from around the world.

In Chapter 1, I said that even if smoking were banned at pipe shows, we would figure out a way around it, and that is what the folks in Chicago did by setting up the circus-like tent next door to the Mega Center, where the actual show is held.

In 2010 Frank Burla retired from his position as head of this show and was succeeded by the estimable Craig Cobine. Craig is Chicago-based attorney who has been involved with the Chicago pipe club for many years.

Two other points that need updating: I mentioned Gary Schrier and his "Confessions" book. He has since founded Briar Books Press, and he offers many pipe books for sale, not only his own but by other authors as well, including reprints of some old English pipe catalogs. The second point involves Neill Archer Roan, who was taking what turned out to be a sabbatical from his website, apassionforpipes.com, at the time that I wrote this article, and is now back at the helm producing frequent blogs on the pipe scene.

One final comment involves the ages of individuals, where, for example, I wrote that "so and so is 50-years-old." Obviously any ages you see were their ages when I wrote this story in 2009.

* * * * *

The Chicago Pipe Show brings out the best in the hobby of pipe collecting: camaraderie, variety, inspiration and enthusiasm. The 2009 show was no exception. In fact, many people said that despite the recession, it was their best show ever.

Having grown up in suburban Chicago, it always brings back special memories when I visit the Windy City.

My wife, Carole, and I flew from Los Angeles and arrived on Wednesday so we could visit with my parents at their assisted living quarters in Evanston, Illinois. On Thursday, we drove our rental car downtown to the restaurant where we had arranged to meet the Danish master pipe maker Lars Ivarsson and his wife, Annette, and Sykes Wilford and Jeff Gracik from the United States.

Sykes is one of the top pipe sellers in the world with his company, smokingpipes.com, and Jeff, whose pipes are known as J. Alan Pipes, is becoming one of the top pipe makers in the world. They represent the future of the hobby at ages 28 and 29 respectively. Another brilliant young pipe maker is Lars's daughter, Nanna, who was unable to attend this year's show because she recently gave birth to a baby boy. She named him "Sixten" after her grandfather, the legendary pipe maker Sixten Ivarsson.

Prior to driving downtown, Jeff had been helping out at the two-day Pipe Making Seminar, which was sold out. Many of the aspiring pipe makers said they could not believe that famous pipe makers took the time to visit the seminar and offer words of advice and support.

I find it encouraging to see so many individuals in their 20s and 30s involved in the hobby today. What makes it so remarkable is that all forms of smoking are considered abhorrent by the culture at large, yet many of these young people are devoting their time and energy to the fascinating world of pipes.

It occurred to me at this year's show, as I gazed around the Mega Center of the Pheasant Run Resort and saw more than a thousand enthusiasts from all over the world, that the profile of each person in the room was incredibly individualistic.

If you were to study the personality profile of a pipe smoker from 50 years ago, you would frequently find a conformist. Pipes were popular and considered a sign of distinction and comfort, and they were often used as props to either look older and wiser, or to fit in with the popular crowd.

Today, pipe smokers are so far off the charts in terms of societal acceptance, or lack thereof, that using the term "nonconformist" does not even scratch the surface. Yet I met at least two dozen new pipe collectors at this year's show who are under 30. Will Purdy, the respected Colorado pipe maker, said that the Denver Pipe Club has suddenly attracted many young people because of Facebook.

I should point out that not all pipe smokers a half century ago were conformists. The ones featured in Pipe Lovers magazine in the 1940s and the collectors who took pride in having dozens, if not hundreds, of pipes were very much like the people who traveled to this year's Chicago Pipe Show. They knew, just like we know, the excitement that beautiful pipes can bring, and like us, they knew and appreciated the relaxing qualities of smoking your favorite blend of tobacco in your favorite pipe.

It is also not unusual to see pipe collectors at shows who have been smoking their pipes for more than half a century, such as the charming Pierre Mueller, 82, from Geneva, Switzerland. I also remember Stan Levi, owner of the Iwan Ries pipe and tobacco store in Chicago, attending the early Chicago shows when he was in his 90s. It is so wonderful that his son, Chuck, and daughter-in-law, Susie, are carrying on the tradition by supporting the show in many ways, including providing an endless supply of hot coffee.

When we were at lunch, enjoying our conversation about pipes, many other pipe show attendees were just down the street visiting Iwan Ries, which has been one of the finest pipe stores in the world for more than a century.

After lunch, we drove to the Pheasant Run Resort, full of anticipation and enthusiasm, and after checking in at the hotel, my first stop was the tent, where we could smoke as many pipe bowls as we wanted while relaxing in lounge chairs or sitting at tables with old and new friends, many of whom were enjoying a buffet of hot and cold food and a full bar.

I had dinner with Neill Archer Roan on Thursday and Saturday nights, and I found his ideas about pipes to be interesting and thought-provoking. Neill was prescient in discovering young American pipe makers such as Adam Davidson, who is 28 and very talented.

At one of our dinners there was another young, and brilliant, pipe maker named Todd Johnson, who recently turned 30. Also at that dinner was the successful eBay pipe seller Rob Cooper of coopersark, energetic Canadian collector Naum Shteinbah, originally from Russia, and Jeff Gracik. What is so interesting about Todd Johnson and Jeff Gracik is that they both earned master's degrees in theology -- Todd at Yale and Jeff at Princeton.

Our discussion was wide-ranging and fascinating, covering topics like pricing strategies for pipe makers and pipe sellers, marketing techniques, what constitutes "plagiarism" in pipe making, should the hobby have "gatekeepers" and any number of related topics.

I wanted to get together with Neill Roan because he has contributed so much to the hobby with his website, "A Passion for Pipes." He kept it going for two years but decided to pull the plug just before the Chicago show. I hope Neill will publish much of his material so everyone interested in the hobby will be able to read it.

Partly because of Neill's writings, I have started buying more pipes made by North American artisans, and in many cases I am struck by the precision, beauty and quality of the work. Just as with the young pipe smokers who attended the show, it is equally remarkable that there are so many talented young pipe makers in this era of no smoking, and they are spread out around the globe. At this year's show I saw beautiful pipes made by Gabriele Dal Fiume from Italy, Alex Florov from Russia (now living in Chicago) and Jürgen Moritz from Germany.

During our dinner discussion, we deliberately focused on areas of disagreement -- hoping to clear the air. No one could disagree with the fact that these young pipe makers are intelligent and articulate, or that Neill and Naum are equally intelligent and articulate. Rob approached the issues from a free market perspective, arguing that pricing is set by the market and changed by the market.

Neill's expertise is marketing strategies and analyses, and I was intrigued when he pointed out that pipe collecting is proceeding along many different paths simultaneously with a wide variety of interests. Only later did I think of the analogy to television, where it has evolved from three or four channels to 500. This is what pipe collecting is like today, with 500 different channels of interest, where you can always find one that appeals to you.

There are Charatan clubs, Castello collectors and diehard Dunhill fans; there are collectors who specialize in Japanese sculptural pipes or Italian straight grains or Danish high grades, North American high grades, German high grades, rare Comoys, GBDs, Custombilts, Sasienis, Kaywoodies or hundreds of other brands. Some collectors limit their pipes to shapes, where they specialize in Calabashes, bulldogs, Canadians or whatever.

There are collectors who refuse to spend more than $20 for a pipe and other collectors who routinely shell out $2,000 for a pipe. It doesn't matter. If you don't like one area of interest, or if you get bored with it, change the channel, and find a different area of interest.

It's all there -- and it was all in Chicago. Of course, there are many collectors who insist on having a wide variety of interests at all times, and that's fine, too. With 306 display tables sold and representatives from 61 countries from around the world, there was no shortage of options for anyone.

Frank Burla is the driving force behind this extravaganza. Frank is a retired FBI agent who devotes his life to making the show a success. He is quick to say that it would not be possible if it weren't for other members of the Chicago Pipe Club who help take care of the thousands of details that go into making the show a success year after year.

I remember visiting Frank at his house in Naperville, Illinois, in 1994 with collector Ed Lehman. At the time, Frank had the largest collection of pipes in the world, with

38,000. He has since, as he puts it, "thinned it down" to a mere 20,000. We were in his remodeled basement, which was the precursor to what has become a pipe museum in his condominium in Downers Grove.

Frank asked me what kind of pipes I liked, and I said Danish and American. He proceeded to bring in giant plastic vats filled to the brim with pipes -- thousands of them. While I was on my hands and knees examining these pieces one at a time, I heard in the background Frank describe to Ed his vision of a new Chicago Pipe Show.

Frank and Dennis DiPiazza had put on some small shows in the 1980s, with Frank organizing the display of antique pipes and Dennis the briars. Frank said he would like to create a whole new kind of show, something much grander and truly international. Ed was very excited about this possibility. I, on the other hand, wasn't paying much attention; I was just thrilled to be on all fours with so many beautiful old pipes on the floor! I bought six, including a Tonni Nielsen "pearl-grade" pipe he had made when he worked at the Larsen factory.

The first of the revised Chicago shows was in 1996, in Rosemont, Illinois, and I remember having a ball. On Sunday afternoon, after the show, I checked out and found a quiet booth in a restaurant, where I poured over old pipe magazines and catalogs I had picked up at the show. I felt so good -- so focused on wanting to collect certain pipes.

Then the show was moved to the Ramada Inn in Harvey, Illinois, where it remained for four years. It was a big deal when Frank announced that the 100-table milestone had been broken. That's why I always get such a kick out of it whenever I hear the occasional grumbler say, "Oh, this show is slow," or words to that effect, when there are literally thousands of offerings.

As the Chicago show grew, it was moved to the Indian Lakes Resort for one year and then the Pheasant Run Resort in St. Charles, Illinois, which is about 45 miles west of downtown Chicago, where it has remained ever since.

One of the ways I gauge attendance is the Friday

night buffet dinner. This is held in a giant ballroom, and it looked to me like nearly every table was filled this year. I sat with the Danish pipe maker Poul Ilsted, famous for making pipes with "facets," and Paul Hildebrand and Andrea Lowe of the Pipe Makers Emporium in Phoenix. They specialize in importing Algerian briar to the United States.

Poul told us that he has spent more than four decades looking at blocks of briar, during those early years working for Eric Nording and at the Larsen pipe factory, and then most of the time for himself. When Poul said he would like to try some Algerian briar, I suggested that I buy some for him on Saturday at the show. I would commission him to make a pipe from one of the blocks, and I will buy that pipe at next year's show.

"That would be fun," he said. "What kind of pipe do you want?"

"Whatever you feel like making," I said.

One reason I gave Poul carte blanch was that last year he had picked out a pipe for me, and it was perfect. We had been smoking our pipes and chatting in the tent when I said that I wanted to buy one of his pipes. We went back into the Mega Center, where he had a dozen pipes on the table. As I was studying each one, Poul picked out a beauty and said, "Here, this is your pipe. It suits you."

The pipe was a faceted straight grain that did indeed fit me perfectly. If you're not clear on what a faceted pipe looks like, picture a pipe with panels on the bowl and a diamond shank, but angled so there is geometric symmetry. If you're still not sure, then Google the name "Poul Ilsted," and look at pictures of his pipes.

Another reason I let Poul decide what shape of pipe to make me is because pipe makers occasionally know better than their customers what pipes the customers will like. Not always, of course. But a number of times over the years I have asked the pipe maker which pipe he would recommend I buy, and I don't ever recall regretting purchasing one of those pipes.

Before going to the pre-show on Friday morning, I had breakfast with hobbyist extraordinaire Rich Esserman of New Jersey (and the New York Pipe Show) and longtime collector Brad McCluskey of St. Louis. We have different interests in the pipes we collect, but what we have in common is our love of pipes. This breakfast has become an annual event, and it is always fun.

We're usually gulping down coffee because we are sleep-deprived, which goes with the territory at pipe shows. Partly this is caused by late-night room hopping, where we look to trade or buy pipes, or just to hang out with each other, or by the late-night socializing and pipe smoking in the tent.

There is another reason why so many of us are sleep-deprived at shows, and it is the same reason children wake up early on Christmas morning. We are so excited to be there! Most of us spend our days with people who have no knowledge of, interest in or understanding of this field that for many of us burns like smoldering embers that never seem to go out. Now, suddenly, we are surrounded by like-minded souls, looking at some of the most beautiful pipes ever made. No wonder we can't sleep!

On Saturday morning I had breakfast with the charming Manduela, a black woman from Denmark who has been a pipe maker with Poul Ilsted for many years and who makes gorgeous miniature pipes. Manduela would later win a large trophy from the pipe smoking contest for being first among the women. Jacques Craen of G. Vincent-Genod Pipes of St. Claude, France, was second in the men's division behind Jeff Weiner of Florida. Both are great guys who just love the hobby.

Joining us at breakfast was Joao Reis, the talented Portuguese pipe maker who lives in Denmark. Several months ago, I bought a Calabash from Joao, and I told him it is too beautiful to smoke. The cap is ivory, and I am afraid of burning it. He and Manduela offered suggestions for lighting it without harming the ivory.

From a buyer's perspective, the actual show was almost anti-climactic because I had spent most of my money on Thursday and Friday, either on pre-orders or on pipes that were too beautiful to turn down, such as a Paolo Becker pipe made out of 2,000-year-old bog oak, known in France as "morta." I've had pencils that weighed more than this pipe.

Naum Shteinbah, the Russian high grade collector who lives in Calgary, introduced me to Sergey Ailarov, another brilliant young pipe maker. The quality of his handwork and staining is spectacular, and I picked up a beautiful little apple. Naum is helping to promote young Russian pipe makers, and I am grateful for that.

My Sergey pipe was in addition to the giant straight-grained apple that Brad Pohlmann had made for me. Brad had a sandblasted version of the pipe at a show in Sparks, Nevada, that Texas collector Mitch Michelson picked up. I asked Brad if he could make me the same pipe as a smooth straight grain. What he made is a work of art, and an unbelievably great smoker.

Speaking of works of art, I picked up this year's Pipes and Tobaccos' "Pipe of the Year" by the American pipe maker Jody Davis. I just love the shape of this pipe, and Jody is truly a master pipe maker.

When I wasn't at the table selling my book, "In Search of Pipe Dreams," I was roaming the Mega Center, trying to examine the contents of each of the tables. I'll bet I didn't even look at a third of them! You'd need a month to really study everything in that room.

This was the first year I stayed over on Sunday night, and I am so glad I did. A large group of pipe enthusiasts, who couldn't get enough of the show, had dinner at a long table in the Harvest restaurant at the resort. I was seated between two of the most intelligent and knowledgeable collectors in the world, Uli Woehrle and Jörg Wittkamp. They have exquisite taste in pipes; no doubt I believe this because we have the same tastes! Uli is a retired pediatrician, and Jörg is a real estate mogul. They both flew in from Germany, and they like to make the Chicago show a weeklong affair.

I was seated across from Tony Soderman, which was fortuitous. Tony and I have locked horns over the issue of "fills vs. flaws," and at dinner we discussed the issue a little and then politely agreed to disagree. I am not prone to writing puns, but I can't resist saying that most readers have had their fill of this issue, so I won't elaborate.

But Tony is an incredibly knowledgeable collector, and we share a bond in having such an intensely passionate love of pipes. We also have some geographical background in common. Tony lives in Minneapolis, and my roots are in Minnesota. My father grew up on a farm in Faribault, Minnesota, which is 40 miles south of Tony's house, and he went to the University of Minnesota. I spent many childhood vacations in Minnesota and, in fact, was there for a family reunion last summer. Tony invited me to visit his house on my next trip to the state, and I am looking forward to that.

This is what is so great about pipe collecting. Here we were, at each other's throats over an issue a few years ago, and now breaking bread together looking for things we have in common, realizing that we really are soul mates.

After dinner we went back to Tony's room so I could study his Kaywoodie collection. Tony is known on the Internet as "Mr. Can" because of his devotion to Canadian-shaped pipes.

This was the first time that I had really studied his pipes at the Chicago show, and I was blown away! The gorgeous shapes and grain of these giant old Kaywoodie Canadians simply cannot be described in words. I also loved the old display cases that Tony has managed to track down over the years.

The pinnacle piece was a carved briar pipe that belonged to the president of Kaywoodie many years ago. The pipe was made between 1932 and 1939 and is more than three feet long ... all one piece of briar! The bowl is four inches tall, and it is kept in the pipe's original fitted velvet case. Tony found this treasure on eBay after endless hours of studying and searching for special Kaywoodies over a period of many years.

The pipe reminded me of a Marxman sculpture made in 1937 that Bruce Harris found at the silent auction of the 2002 Chicago Pipe Show and shared with us this year. This is the same pipe that was featured several times in the old Pipe Lover's magazine. It had come from the museum collection of Frank Burla.

Bruce's pipe was in the glass display cabinet next to John Tolle's specially commissioned "Lord of the Rings" pipes made by Michael Parks of Canada. The sculpture on these pipes was breathtaking.

There were two other glass cabinet display cases filled with gorgeous old Calabash pipes, many of which were made more than a hundred years ago. They were from the collections of John Fabris and Gary Schrier, who incidentally has written a new bestselling pipe book to accompany his earlier book about Calabash pipes. The new book is called "Confessions of a Pipeman," and it was offered for sale at the show.

Can you imagine the fun Tony, Bruce, John Tolle, Michael, John Fabris and Gary had in pursuing their own pipe dreams over the years? And can you imagine what it was like for Tony and Bruce when they hit the jackpot and got such extraordinary pieces after so many years of searching? Can you imagine the satisfaction Michael felt after completing his unbelievably beautiful sculptures, or the thrill John got when he first saw them? The same for John Fabris and Gary Schrier, where the discovery of each of their dozens of Calabash gems was a cause for celebration.

Now you're starting to see why pipe collecting is so much fun, and why so many pipe collectors feel so intensely enthusiastic about the hobby. And these are only a few of the 500 channels of interest that are available to all collectors.

For myself, I have focused on beautiful pipes made by individual artisans. I have also spent an enormous amount of time reading and writing about pipes, and on experimenting with the internal design of pipes, studying the ones I like and trying to have their specifications made uniform (though that is not always wise). In addition, I am passionate about restoring and cleaning old pipes to make them look like new. The late Jim Benjamin's enthusiasm for this "channel" was contagious.

After leaving Tony's room, we walked across the hall to "Brother Dave's" room, where he was serving his famous Cuban coffee, after-dinner liquors and some delicious tobacco carefully aged since the 1950s. We were packed in like sardines, and we loved it! Brother Dave is David Sahagian of Detroit, and he is a kind and loving pipe collector who makes everything fun. He embodies benevolence and good times; hence his nickname.

Karin and Mimmo from Italy, who provide briar to pipe makers and who make pipes themselves, were there, along with the Americans Marty Pulvers and Andrew Marks -- Marty being a charismatic pipe seller and friend of the hobby for many decades, and Andrew being a great American pipe maker. I sat on the window ledge next to Gabriele Dal Fiume. We were both enjoying our pipes, sharing this common bond of friendship.

I saw people from Russia, Germany, Italy, Switzerland, Belgium, Denmark and the United States -- all crammed into one small hotel room. Jörg Wittcamp observed, "This looks like a United Nations conference."

I have often stated that I collect pipes for fun and for no other reason, and I had more fun this year than you can imagine. What I want most out of the hobby is precisely what a good pipe show gives me. At Chicago this year, I met so many old friends and made so many new ones, that it was difficult to keep track.

Maya Angelou once said, "I've learned that people will forget what you said, people will forget what you did, but people will never forget how you made them feel."

A good pipe show will make you feel like I felt when I left Chicago. It is what Ed Lehman described as being "filled up" -- a feeling of warmth, good cheer and love -- all revolving around an activity that is increasingly being prohibited and censored. No wonder pipe collecting is gaining in popularity.

CHAPTER FOUR

~~~~~

FAVORITE PIPE OF THE DAY

This chapter was inspired by the writer and pipe aficionado, Christopher Morley, who wrote an essay nearly a century ago about his favorite pipe of the day.

For most people, coffee is best enjoyed in the morning and alcohol in the evening. Many other beverages and foods, pastimes and activities, all lend themselves to a natural time of day that makes the most sense. But when it comes to relaxing with your pipe, it can be at any time of day or night.

This chapter is from an article that I wrote for the Pipe Smoker's Ephemeris in 2004 showing the results of my questioning 16 experienced pipe smokers about what time of day lends itself to be the best time to enjoy a pipe. In fact, assuming an average of 30 years' experience as pipe smokers for each survey participant (which is probably on the low side), we are talking about something like a combined total of 500 years of pipe smoking experience! What is not surprising is that each participant had a definite opinion about the best time of day to enjoy a pipe, and very few were in agreement.

However, it is important to point out that our tastes change over time, and it is entirely possible that many of the individuals interviewed for this chapter would today disavow their comments from 2004 and cite an entirely different time of day for their favorite pipe. That is yet another benefit of the pipe -- the flexibility that comes from experimentation. Someone whose favorite pipe was at the crack of dawn just after getting out of bed might now say that his favorite pipe is just before retiring to bed late at night.

* * * * *

What is your favorite pipe of the day? An informal survey of more than a dozen experienced pipe smokers shows that we're all over the map when it comes to describing our favorite pipe of the day. I conducted this survey over a period of months in 2004 and discovered that if there was one theme or common denominator, it was this: Most pipe smokers these days smoke their pipes as a form of meditation -- a relaxing break in each 24-hour day, whether first thing in the morning, last thing at night or any time in between.

Collector Leonard Fogel of Scarsdale, New York, pointed out that in the 1950s, anyone could smoke pretty much anywhere they wanted. But today, with the ubiquitous "no smoking" signs, we are limited to fewer pipe bowls per day, so we relax and savor them more than ever.

"Pipe smoking was never intended to be a rushed event," said Fogel, a pipe collector for three decades. "It is, fundamentally, a contemplative endeavor."

Len spoke for nearly every pipe smoker surveyed when he said, "If you have the time and location to comfortably listen to great music, read or watch an old movie, the pipe you smoke on this occasion will likely be your favorite of the day."

In one of the old black-and-white Sherlock Holmes movies, featuring Basil Rathbone as Holmes and Nigel Bruce as Dr. Watson, both men agree that their favorite pipe is the one they enjoy first thing in the morning. When I have the time, which is usually only on Sunday mornings, I like to sit in my den, drink coffee, smoke a pipe, read the paper and listen to classical music, with my German Shepherd lying next to my chair. There is something so relaxing about waking up this way -- I just wish I could do it every day!

Steve Fallon of Waco, Texas, has figured out how to make this an everyday practice, and I am envious of his morning routine, which he describes as follows:

"As the director of a nonprofit museum, my job requires much fundraising and public relations work as well as putting on special events. In addition, I am a part-time radio and television sports broadcaster. Balancing both jobs requires putting in a lot of hours each day and frequently being around a lot of people. Private time is tough to find. Fortunately, I am an early riser and spend the first hour of every day in happy seclusion with my pipe, a couple of cups of strong coffee, my Bible and the morning newspaper. My wife says she believes the sports section of the newspaper is really my Bible.

"My routine is simple. Before retiring for the evening, I select a pipe from my rack in my home office. I then set it in the holder on my pipe ashtray located on the coffee table in the den next to my recliner. A tin of Dunhill's Royal Yacht is a permanent fixture there as well.

"When the morning alarm goes off, I get out of bed and garner a bit of exercise by jogging to the coffee pot in the kitchen. While the coffee is brewing I sit in my recliner, which is located by the fireplace, and start loading my pipe with Royal Yacht (a nicotine-laden Virginia blend that I truly believe was the Nectar of the Gods.) It is rich, smooth and contains a spine-tingling casing that is delicious. Once my briar is packed to perfection, I get my first cup of coffee, return to my recliner and get that pipe lit! For the first fifteen minutes of my private hour I do nothing but alternate sips of coffee with sips of tobacco. Heaven on earth! The next half hour or so is spent perusing the newspaper and then having a little meditation time. All the while smoking my pipe and thoroughly enjoying the start of my day. So now you know that I mean it when I say I can't wait until tomorrow!"

Per Billhall of Gothenburg, Sweden, also cited his first pipe of the day as his favorite. "Sitting with my laptop with my new family member, the lab puppy 'Benson,' at my feet, reading the night's mail, having a cup of coffee, keeping one eye on the morning television news and reading the paper -- the morning smoke is something special," Per said. "A typical pipe is a blasted Stanwell straight pipe filled with Capstan Mild -- the more sophisticated combinations I save for later in the day ..."

Another European, Jan Andersson, publisher of the Swedish pipe magazine Rokringar and author of two fantastic books about pipes, also cites his first pipe of the day as one of his two favorites -- the other being in the evening. Jan explains: "After I have had my breakfast, I take a cup of coffee and my daily paper to the den, sit down in my favorite chair and fill the first pipe of the day. I prefer a medium-strong Virginia, not too strong but not harmless either -- I want to be satisfied. Of course, this first pipe of the day is especially appreciated on a free day, when I might be sitting in my den for more than an hour, just enjoying life.

"My other favorite pipe is in the evening. After work and having had my supper, I again take a cup of coffee to my den to relax. Usually I prefer a Latakia mixture or, occasionally, a Virginia or Burley flake. I often have a conversation with my wife about the day passed or something else, or, if she is busy, I read a book or do a crossword. I may also watch a program on the TV, but that is not very common. A dark, cold evening, just like the ones we are having now here in Sweden, is a perfect complement to this second favorite pipe of the day."

Retired attorney John Goldberg of Chicago, a collector for many decades, said that he too savors his first pipe of the day. "My favorite pipe of the day is the pipe I smoke after breakfast," John said. "Since retirement, my post-breakfast pipe is enjoyed in my den -- upon entering my den you surely realize that a pipe smoker is in residence. The walls are decorated with posters created by Bob Watson for the Chicago pipe shows, old pipe advertising and a caricature of my wife and me -- and pipes are displayed along with a number of cans of tobacco. My first job is to choose -- sometimes a pipe will call out to be smoked -- sometimes my choice of tobacco will dictate which pipe to reach for -- so many choices ...

"Having chosen, I retire to my easy chair -- a leather Ez-boy -- to my right there is a table containing a mug of coffee, ashtray, Butera pipe rest, pipe cleaners, wooden matches and a tamper, while to my left there sits a reading lamp and another table suitable to rest a book or magazine. In front of me and along the wall are pipe cases, a dresser containing pipes and tobaccos, a stereo and a television. To read or meditate, that is my choice, and very often choosing to meditate on the issues of my day, the match is struck, the first charring light and the taste of the tobacco, tamp and relight, and once the tobacco is burning properly, I think about the 24 hours ahead as I watch the smoke rise in the air. I examine the pipe I am smoking: its shape, grain, how it feels in my hand -- today it's a Butera Royal Classic quarter-bent apple with beautiful straight grain filled with golden cake Virginia -- and I know that God's in His heaven and all is right with my world."

Another Chicago attorney, Ed Lehman, is an avid Dunhill collector. He said his favorite pipes are smoked when he walks downtown in the Loop from the train station to his office, tamping his tobacco and lighting his pipe at traffic lights, nodding in a friendly way when he sees an occasional pipe smoker.

"I've done this for many years and thought nothing of it," he said. "But in the last few years I have noticed that very few other pipe smokers are on the streets. And I get a kick out of the different reactions of people when they see my pipe. Some appear to love it, and some do not. I always chuckle when an anti-smoker makes a pretend cough. Here we are in Chicago, with all the cars, buses and pollution you can imagine, and this guy is bothered by my pure Virginia blend. It is so silly, you have to laugh. The irony of it all makes this one my favorite pipe of the day, and you never know what reaction you'll find."

Albert Mendez of New York, who wrote the brilliant Introduction and Epilogue to "In Search of Pipe Dreams," offered a unique interpretation of my question, which he said evoked some very happy memories, and he focused on the place as well as time for his favorite pipe. "Favorite place and time to smoke a pipe? This is a difficult question to answer," he said, "but the one place and time I constantly remember, is the garden of my old house, here in Flushing, New York, where Jacqueline and I lived when we were in the United States, four or five months out of the year.

"The house was a center-hall, pseudo-Colonial, untouched since it was built in the early twenties. It had a long garden, stretching back to the next street, not manicured at all, but more like a piece of parkland, with nice old trees, shrubs, and English ivy ground cover. I spent a great deal of time in this garden, cutting firewood for the fireplaces (our main source of heat, for aesthetic reasons, and because the heating system did not work very well.) After one or two hours of splitting and cutting, Jackie would bring me out a cup of coffee (the black Cuban stuff, in tiny cups) and then I would sit inside this old wheelbarrow that we had picked up in a Cape Cod antique shop, cover myself with a moth-eaten plaid (that Jackie used for picnics as a child), and smoke Troost slices (the only non-English mixture that I have ever smoked) in a 'shop' pipe. This pipe (and this tobacco) was smoked only out there, and only after cutting firewood. Don't ask me why, 'cause I can't explain it.

"Anyways, this is the one time and place that I remember being perfectly happy, in that cold and perfectly still garden, surrounded by old trees and shrubs, with that damp, heavy feeling in the air that you get just before a snowfall, and the aroma of the Troost lingering around me. Of course, I can't have been perfectly happy, because the human condition does not allow for that, but I remember it that way."

I need to make a comment about Albert's last sentence because it would appear to be so contrary to my own sense of life. As you can tell from my writings, it is hard to imagine a more optimistic, enthusiastic and passionate pipe collector than I am, yet I absolutely love Albert's resignation and caustic comments about the futility of life in these modern times. I'm not sure why, but I suspect it has something to do with the fact that Albert feels passionately about all of his views, and in that sense we are soul mates. In addition, we are in total agreement in passionately disliking many of the developments of the modern world; for example, communism and all forms of statism that call for one group controlling everyone else. But now, let's get back to the best-time-of-day question.

Chuck Stanion, editor of Pipes and Tobaccos magazine, prefers his mid-day pipe as his favorite: "My favorite pipe of the day? Gosh, that's a tough one. It's definitely not the first pipe of the day, because I smoke that one on the drive to work in rush hour traffic. It helps keep me sane and calm, for sure, and has the added bonus of keeping me from exchanging hand gestures with other drivers, most of whom seem intent on killing me. I once forgot myself and stuck my fist out the car window to shake at a soccer mom who cut me off on I-40 for no apparent reason other than to try to tear off a piece of my front bumper for a souvenir. Unfortunately, the fist I shook out the window had an Eltang billiard in it, and I dropped it. I immediately felt the error of my ways as I watched in the rear view mirror as that wonderful pipe tumbled under the tires of an oncoming tractor-trailer that wanted me out of its lane.

"The last pipe of the day is very nice, but it gets me in trouble sometimes. I have that one after the rest of the family has gone to bed and I have the night to myself to sit in front of the fire, on cold nights, or on the deck during nice weather. The problem is that the last pipe of the day sometimes keeps me up too late. It's hard to let that mellow, relaxing final pipe go out. That last pipe sometimes requires a payoff in the form of next-day exhaustion and rush-hour intolerance. Usually it's worth it, but I think we've all paid the price at one time or another, and it can be tough.

"The after-dinner pipe used to be a favorite, but not these days. That's the hour now that I spend helping my daughter with her homework, and though I always have a pipe going, the challenges of third-grade math make me excitable -- I puff too hard and don't pay attention to the tobacco. It does provide the pauses in calculation that are necessary to make my daughter think I really know what I'm doing as I silently count my fingers and toes to figure out a problem while I'm tamping and lighting and trying to look intelligent. It's a lifesaver, but it is not the best pipe of the day.

"I think my favorite smoke is the one that follows lunch. If it has been a stressful business lunch, one comprised of people trying to get me to do things I don't want to do, the pipe relaxes me; it puts life back into perspective and lets me do something I do want to do. If it's been an enjoyable social lunch, the pipe is the perfect dessert for it and extends the contentment. The day is still young after lunch, so I'm not stressed about how much there is yet to accomplish. I can gather my thoughts, enjoy the tobacco and make a plan for the afternoon. I can concentrate on the tobacco and the pipe, enjoy what they both offer and feel good about it. Yes, that's my favorite. Now I need to find a way to have lunch several times a day."

Another professional writer and pipe collector is Bill Unger, who edits The Pipe Collector newsletter. He too prefers that mid-day pipe above all others. "I have various favorite smokes and times, but I guess that one of my most favorites occurs after I've been working at my desk all morning and it's time for lunch," Bill said. "I'll make a simple one and eat it at my desk, reading whatever book I'm reading at the time (for a while, it was yours). Then I'll make myself a cup of tea or coffee, fill up, usually, one of my favorite David Jones pipes with McClelland 2015 or McCranies' Southport (both matured Virginias with Perique), and smoke, drink, and read for a half hour or so until it's time to go back to work."

Bruce Harris, the Marxman collector who has written many fascinating articles about pipe collecting and pipe smoking, said that his favorite bowl comes a little later in the day -- just after work. Initially, Bruce wrote that his favorite pipe was one he smoked to celebrate some good news, but then he revised his comments as follows: "In thinking about your question of 'favorite pipe,' I'm changing my mind. It isn't fair to call a celebratory smoke a favorite. By definition, one feels good during a celebration. The pipe just enhances that feeling.

"On a day-to-day basis, I would have to say the 'after work,' or 'the drive home pipe,' is my favorite time to smoke. I have an hour commute home. Time to relax and unwind, open the collar, turn on the radio, and light up. This is especially true in the Fall and Winter seasons. I like to listen to sports games and sports talk radio stations. The stress of the day simply flows away. Alone in my car, the workplace behind me and home in front of me. Thoughts of seeing my family and eating dinner take over. Every now and then I will see someone else smoking a pipe and driving. There is an immediate bond that takes place between the two of us. You can't help but smile and raise your pipe."

Dr. Eric Hesse, a psychology professor at the University of California at Berkeley, said it is easy to identify his favorite pipe bowl of the day because he only smokes one a day. "My favorite pipe of the day is usually my only pipe of the day," he said. "Although I have about 100 pipes, nine times out of ten, in the late afternoon, I smoke one of the 20 of my pre-1960s Dunhill LB's. This is the time of day when work is slowing down and the pipe helps me slow down. An LB will normally smoke for me for about two hours (I'm slow). I like a two-hour pipe for a 'regular smoke' (although I'm smoking a very large 'Teddy' horn at the moment). There's something about the old LB's which to me represents the essential, basic PIPE. Late afternoon, a little sun coming in through the window and the smoke of a fine Virginia rising in the air. That is my favorite pipe of the day."

Several other collectors cited that first pipe after work as their favorite. Interestingly, two are medical doctors -- Mark Beale of South Carolina and Jörg Lehman of Ulm, Germany (formerly East Germany). Here are Dr. Lehman's comments: "I am a professor of fundamentals in medicine at the University of Applied Sciences here in my home town. I have many lessons a day, and, of course, I cannot smoke during this period. In addition, sometimes these many lessons lead to back pain. For that reason, my best time for the first relaxed puffs is in the afternoon, when I am back in my office.

"I will start my computer, fill my pipe with my favorite tobacco (Ennerdale Flake, made by Gawith Hoggarth), while it boots, and then I start smoking and reading my pipe-related correspondence. I prefer to smoke a smaller, slightly bent freehand pipe with a higher bowl, made by Cornelius Mänz. This pipe has a comfortable bite and is so well balanced, that I can hold it in my mouth for a longer timespan.

"When I am back home, there are waiting always some interesting pipes. During the evening, I prefer to smoke the pipes I have acquired recently. For the moment, this includes a pipe made by Tony Rodriguez, a large chimney made by J.T. Cooke and a giant freehand made by Jess Chonowitsch. It is always very interesting to have some new pipes, but waiting for the right moment to start smoking is important."

Dr. Beale's favorite pipe is one of those that "lets the air out," as Ed Kolpin put it. Kolpin, founder of the original Tinder Box, maintained that "you live longer with a pipe" because it is such a marvelous way to cope with stress, and he lived to be 97. He was an evangelist in spreading his gospel of the importance of using your pipe to help you relax and lower your blood pressure.

Mark wrote that as a psychiatrist, he is often asked if he gets tired of hearing patients complain all the time. "'Don't you get fed up with people whining at you for eight hours a day?' people ask. Rather than feeling that my patients are a group of complainers, I am continually struck by the degree of misfortune many face in their lives. So many of us are so very lucky and do not realize it.

"Helping people deal with life's most intense struggles is draining, however. At the end of a long day, like a carpenter with a sore shoulder, my psyche is exhausted. Upon arriving home from work, the lighting of a pipe allows me to re-set my emotional thermostat. Whether it be a Danish straight grain or a Julius Vesz Hand Cut briar filled with a Dunhill Latakia mixture, smoking a pipe of tobacco revives me, rejuvenates me, and re-invigorates me every evening. In truth, I don't know what I would do without it.

"My favorite pipe of the day is also my first, smoked alone before dinner. It begins in silence, then after a few minutes I will either listen to Kenny Burrell jazz guitar or turn on the tube if I think I can stomach the news. Often, I will eventually make it to my computer to answer my email before the bowl burns out. Then comes dinner and another bowlful of a Latakia blend before bed."

Ken Campbell, a collector from Wheeling, WV, offers comments similar to those made by Christopher Morley in his 1918 book, Shandygaff. Morley wrote that he savored his after-breakfast pipe, but since his mind was not fully awake, his senses could not appreciate it as much as they did later in the day.

In an essay entitled, "The Last Pipe," Morley wrote that nothing compares with the last pipe of the day, smoked while reading the General Catalogue of the Oxford University Press.

"With due care I fill, pack, and light the last pipe of the day, to be smoked reverently and solemnly in bed," Morley wrote. "The thousand brain-murdering interruptions are over. The gentle sibilance of air drawn through the glowing nest of tobacco is the only sound. With reposeful heart I turn to some favourite entry in my well-loved catalogue. One o'clock is about to chime in the nearby steeple, but my pipe and curiosity are now both going strong …"

Like Christopher Morley, Ken Campbell prefers his pipes after he is fully awake and when he can relax and concentrate on enjoying the experience. "For me, the best pipe of the day is not a function of time but rather a function of conditions," Ken said. "By 'conditions,' I mean the condition of my palate and the availability of time to concentrate solely on my smoking. My palate is almost always way off the mark in the early morning. Hence my breakfast pipe is never my best pipe of the day. During the rest of the day, I am usually working at my desk. Therefore, the second condition is not met during work, although I do smoke off and on while at work, but I never derive full enjoyment from it.

"I like to devote a few uninterrupted hours to my pipe. During that time, I do not read, or converse. I concentrate on my pipe and my smoking to the exclusion of everything else. I attempt to refine my sense of taste, perfect my ability to blow smoke rings, and to smoke very slowly, at the same time keeping the pipe lit.

"I do not have a chance to indulge my ideal every day, but when I do, the pleasure, enjoyment, and relaxation that my pipe affords me are from another world."

Richard Carleton Hacker is the author of numerous excellent pipe books, including "Pipesmoking -- A 21st Century Guide" and "Rare Smoke." Hacker's reply was similar to Jan Andersson's of Sweden, in that he has more than one favorite pipe of the day. "Actually, I have two favorite times to smoke a pipe each day. One, if deadlines permit, is in the mid-afternoon. When most people take a coffee break, I take a pipe break. It helps me relax and sort things out, freeing me from the 'real world,' if you will. My second pipe break -- and actually a ritual that I rarely miss, even when I'm traveling -- is at the end of the day, late at night, when my work is done, the phone is silent, and I'm too tired to write or think about another word. That's when one of my favorite big-bowled briars comes out, I fill it with an English blend, pour a snifter of malt whiskey, and let the cares of the day dissipate like so many swirls of smoke."

Rich Esserman, a frequent contributor to The Pipe Smoker's Ephemeris, also prefers to smoke in the evening. "Years ago, when I lived in upstate New York, I was able to smoke quite a number of bowls a day," he said. "This was due to the fact that I lived five minutes from work and could go home during lunch, plus I was single and could smoke in my own place at my leisure. Now I work in a very smoker unfriendly city -- namely New York City -- and my commute is about one-and-a-half hours each way. So the only real opportunity I get to smoke during the week is in the evenings, and then I like to smoke one long bowl.

"I have expanded my collection greatly (for me at least) to 150 pipes. Currently, I have a wide variety of extra large pipes that include old and new Dunhill Magnums, Castello standard shapes and freehands and a number of Danish makers such as Bo Nordh, Tom Eltang, Chonowitsch and Bang that also are in a combination of standard and freehand shapes. I do not have a rotation per se but smoke whatever hits my fancy. There are times when I am interested in smoking giant bents, other times only a beautiful freehand will do. I do have a tendency to 'pair up' my pipes so I always smoke certain pipes back-to-back.

"I smoke down in my basement area. The surroundings where I smoke have never been important to me. Usually I am writing or reading when I smoke, so when I light up a bowl I am transported to some other place and time."

Greg Pease, who sells outstanding pipe tobaccos under the name G.L. Pease, offered these thoughts: "Any time of day is a great time to enjoy the pleasures of the pipe, but for me, it's the stillness and darkness of night that bring out the best that a favorite briar and blend have to offer. With dinner behind me, and the concerns of the day having followed the sun to sink below the horizon, all that is left is to settle in with a pipe and my thoughts. My mind is free to swirl and slow-dance with the wisps of smoke that rise from the bowl, perfuming the air with a wonderful fragrance.

"During the day, I'm too often inclined to devour the smoke, puffing as though my desire is to finish the bowl as soon as possible. At night, though, I'll take delicious sips, savoring each one, hoping to keep the embers alive forever, as though trying to delay the inevitability of the rising sun, and the start of a new day. Too soon, the bowl will be finished. Too soon, the sun will rise. But, in those moments of late night solitude, shared only with my pipe, I can almost feel eternity."

Regis McAfferty is another pipe smoking writer, whose three outstanding books -- "Bugs," "Then...Now...Whenever..." and "Another View From The Park" -- were all published during the past 12 months. McAfferty's remarks about his favorite pipe of the day are reminiscent of Christopher Morley's. "Next to my bed on the nightstand are two items that provide the greatest pleasure for me at the end of each day: a book, usually a collection of eighteenth century stories, or some history of England; and a two-pipe stand with two pipes resting on it. Though it may seem a paradox, my last pipe of the day is always Early Morning Pipe tobacco. I find it deliciously rich and satisfying, absent of the heavier note of stronger Latakia blends, and after a half hour's reading, can drift off to sleep with the aroma of that fine English blend lingering in the air, leading me often to dreams of yesteryear. I have ended each day's waking hours in the same manner for so long, I can't remember when I began, but for me, there is no finer pipe of the day."

The main point for me is that each of the individuals who were interviewed for this chapter use their pipe as a form of relaxation, regardless of time of day. Your pipe will help you enjoy each day more by providing an easy wake-up call in the morning, a gentle soothing during the day, or serene contemplation as you unwind at night. Your pipe has all the bases covered, and your only job is to find out what works best for you.

CHAPTER FIVE

~~~~~

PIPE SHAPES FROM THE FARMERS MARKET

Clockwise from the top: a tomato by Bo Nordh; an egg by Sixten Ivarsson; a peach by Jess Chonowitsch; a strawberry by Nanna Ivarsson, and an apple by S. Bang.

This brief essay and beautiful photograph first appeared in Pipes and Tobaccos magazine in the Winter edition of 2004.

* * * * *

All pipe makers are artists as well as craftsmen, and many draw inspiration for their pipe shapes from nature. We have seen pipes shaped liked tulips, snails, blowfish, hawkbills and countless other natural creations. There are also pipes shaped after man-made objects, such as a pot, an iron or a brandy glass.

Some of the shapes that I find the most intriguing, probably because they are so basic, are shapes modeled after foods. These are usually foods that we can hold in our hands, just like a pipe. (Obviously the eggs should be in the shell or hard boiled!)

So when I met with professional photographer Bob Gardner in Los Angeles, I asked if he could take a photograph of some of my pipes with shapes that look like they came from the Farmers Market. I told Bob and his wife, Gail, that the shapes were an egg, a tomato, apple, peach and a strawberry, and asked if they could guess which was which.

They had never heard of any of the pipe makers, but they correctly matched all five pipes to the designated shapes immediately, without any hesitation. Then Bob displayed them on a dark green felt cloth in his photo studio and took the picture.

~~~~~

CHAPTER SIX

ODE TO PIPE COLLECTING

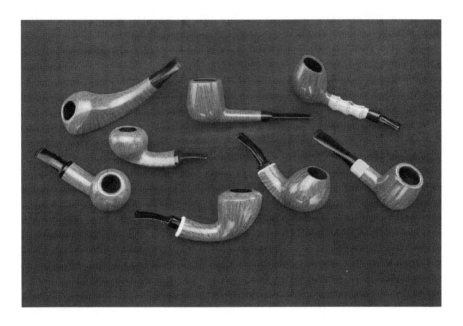

It makes me feel good to thank my favorite pipe makers, such as Jess Chonowitsch, for making such beautiful pipes.

When this chapter was written in October 2006 for *The Pipe Collector* newsletter, it created controversy -- a real firestorm of protest over the issue of fills in pipes. The next issue of the publication was dominated by many pages of scathing criticism of Bo Nordh and me, though we had our defenders as well. My only response at the time appears in the first part of the next chapter.

But for this chapter I decided to rewrite certain sections of my controversial essay because the criticism forced me to learn as much as possible about fills, and at a later date I will write a detailed article on this topic, but for now I have deleted mention of it. I will only say that there is a difference between plugging up a hole in the wood versus stabilizing the outside surface of a briar bowl so that the soft parts of the wood become just as hard a surface as the rest of the bowl -- so that the entire bowl has a consistently hard surface. I believe that this is what caused the confusion in the first place, and it is a topic that I intend to write about in depth at a future date.

I do want to point out that the resentment was so intense at the time that two readers even chastised me for using the word "ode" without then offering a lyric poem. They said that, by definition, an ode must always be a lyric poem. I remember thinking, "Tell that to the editors of The New York Times" and others because the word "ode" is routinely used in newspaper headlines as a form of tribute, always followed by prose and never a lyric poem. However, I checked three different dictionaries, and sure enough, they all said it must be a "lyric poem." So then I contacted the editors of several dictionaries, showing them the newspaper examples, and they said they would correct future editions to reflect modern usage of the word.

Pipe collecting has made my life so much richer, and I try to communicate that throughout this book, but especially in this chapter, which is why I wanted to pay tribute to the people who are responsible for creating, and supporting, a world of beauty through pipes.

* * * * *

I became a pipe collector because I love pipes. I love everything about them. I attend pipe shows and read pipe magazines because of the camaraderie and good spirit that I have found over the years with like-minded collectors who share my passion for pipes -- their beauty, design, engineering, smoking qualities and the memories I associate with them. Borrowing a sentiment from John Haloftis, the prolific pipe author from Greece, my pipes are some of my best friends.

But I have noticed a disturbing trend during the past few years, where some collectors are attacking the choices of other collectors, where smokers of one brand of pipes criticize other brands of pipes and individual pipe makers. Some even criticize the pipe makers whose pipes they buy.

I see this as a potentially dangerous development. You have to remember that everything is changing at warp speed, and this profoundly affects pipe collecting, both good and bad. The world has become a very small place because of the availability of low-fare air travel and iPhones, Blackberries, iPads, iPods, Kindles, laptops, Facebook, Twitter and other forms of social media as well as many other products and devices of the digital age. One consequence of this instant communication is that reputations can be damaged easily, where false rumors can travel around the world in a matter of hours.

Another consequence is that the anti-smoking movement is galloping across the globe at an accelerating pace. It has become unpopular to smoke, whether in California, New York, Indiana or even in Ireland, Denmark and France. Pipes and cigars are lumped with mass-marketed cigarettes, and all smoking is criticized or even condemned. We can't smoke in restaurants. We can't smoke in bars. We can't smoke at the office. We can't smoke at many hotels. We can't smoke in public, and we consider ourselves lucky if we can smoke in private.

We have all experienced disapproval from our friends,

family and associates. I suspect most of you are like me, where we ignore, or rebel against, this onslaught.

We all know there are risks associated with excessive tobacco use. The keys to a lifetime of enjoyment are moderation and not inhaling. Some of us believe that moderate pipe use can actually provide health benefits because of its stress-reducing qualities. But we are clearly in a minority at this time.

However, there are many pluses to this globalization as well. The biggest one is the instant availability of what used to be hard-to-find products. We are able to buy our favorite pipes any day of the week, usually on the Internet, but also occasionally by traveling to pipe shows or by visiting our favorite pipe stores, even if they are many miles from home.

In October 2006, I was fortunate to visit Copenhagen for two days and spend some time with some of my favorite pipe makers, and in light of Bo Nordh's death the previous July, this visit held special significance. I savored each minute I was able to spend with Jess Chonowitsch, Lars Ivarsson, Ulf Noltensmeier and Per Hansen.

My wife and I flew from Prague to Copenhagen early on a Friday morning, and I had lunch with Per and Ulf on Friday, and with Lars and Jess on Saturday. The best part about the meetings was that I was able to thank these Old World master artisans for all the contentment they have given me. They have enriched my life immeasurably by making such beautiful pipes -- pipes that I have enjoyed over and over for years, and will be able to enjoy for the rest of my life.

This is a very important point that I believe is too often overlooked as a growing number of collectors try to score "gotcha!" points in finding fault with one brand of pipe or another. It's much healthier to focus on what you like and to savor your enjoyment of your own pipes.

It makes no difference if you prefer Dunhill, Barling, Kaywoodie, Ser Jacopo, Poul Ilsted, Bo Nordh, Mark Tinsky, Julius Vesz, Custombilt, Charatan, Castello, Baldo

Baldi, Savinelli, Peterson, Jim Cooke or any other brand of pipe, whether it be from a factory or an individual.

This is what you like, and this is what you should enjoy. If it is a contemporary pipe maker, try to get to know him. Visit a pipe show where the pipe maker might be, so you can have a chance to ask questions and maybe special-order a pipe. Or if you can't make a show, then Google the pipe maker's name and you're likely to find his website, or his dealer's website, and you can start corresponding by e-mail with the pipe maker or his distributor. If your favorites are older pipes that are no longer made, it is a great deal of fun to research those pipes, and the Internet has made it easy to pursue leads. There are plenty of other pipe enthusiasts who will be happy to help you.

I have been helped by expert collectors many times over the years. One time during the Chicago Pipe Show, I met with John Loring, Rich Esserman and Monica McGregor, daughter of the late collector Ed Lehman, who helped me more times than I can count. As we looked over Ed's pipe collection, which was about to be sold, John Loring made a casual statement to Monica that was really quite profound: "You can't imagine how much pleasure, how much fun and enjoyment, these pipes gave your father."

And Monica knew this was true. "Yes, he really did love his pipes," she said. "He just loved everything about pipe collecting."

Rich Esserman and I chatted (too) briefly during this year's Richmond show, and we both commented on how much we still miss Ed Lehman. I feel indebted to both John Loring and Rich Esserman because I always learn from them, especially when it comes to tobacco. John teases me about my love of high-grade Danish pipes, but that's OK, because it is always good natured. Also, one of my favorite Sixten Ivarsson pipes was acquired when I traded John a 1940s Dunhill plus some other items. That was more than a dozen years ago at an Indiana Briar Friars show, and I was always impressed that John knew enough to have acquired the Ivarsson pipe in the first place -- even if he would use it to trade for a Dunhill.

But that's the point. John loves Dunhill, while I love Ivarsson, and we get along fine. Neither one of us spends a nanosecond trying to find fault with each other's choices.

As for Rich Esserman, he is arguably the most knowledgeable person I've ever met when it comes to pipe collecting. He is like a sponge that keeps absorbing new facts and theories about pipes and tobaccos. I can't ever remember asking Rich a question that he wasn't able to help me with the answer.

One of the things I like best about Rich is his lack of dogmatism as a collector. He is always curious, known for his Dunhill magnums, but he is also an expert on Castello pipes, and he wrote recently about enjoying his Bo Nordh pipes.

The key is to find what you like, whether it is one brand or many brands. Find what "gives you pleasure, what makes collecting fun," to paraphrase John Loring, and pursue your hobby with a passion. If you don't like a particular brand, or if it is out of your price range, then ignore it and find what you do like and are able to afford.

My hope is that all pipe collectors will focus on what is most important to them in their pipe collecting, and that they will avoid attacking any pipe maker they might not like. Spend your time praising and enjoying the pipes that you like, and your pipe collecting hobby will be much more fun. My only reason for being a pipe collector is to have fun, and I don't find it fun when the focus is on the negative. As Jess Chonowitsch said after a flap involving Bo Nordh, "There are so few of us pipe smokers left, it's really in our interest to get along."

Over the years I have written hundreds of thousands of words about pipes and pipe collecting, and I don't ever recall criticizing a pipe maker -- at least I hope I haven't, and I hope I never will in the future. When I think about how hard each pipe maker works to produce his best pipes, I get apoplectic when I read off-hand attacks on any pipe maker. These attacks are especially prevalent today on

Internet chat lines, on various forms of social media, in casual e-mails and in group conversations at pipe shows. I always think of the saying, "Any mule can kick down a barn."

However, I feel compelled to restrict my comments to pipe makers as artisans, as opposed to pipe makers as salesmen. I find that some of the newer pipe makers use what feel like high pressure sales tactics, and that is unfortunate. I'm sure they don't mean to be offensive, but just the fact that they are pushing their own products places an awkward pressure on us collectors. I am not alone in making this observation. Many other collectors have told me they feel the same way. I believe every pipe maker should focus on making pipes and let professional pipe dealers do their selling. The dealers can build the brand, promote the pipe maker's work, and even absorb criticism that they can pass along in a constructive way. I think it is fine for a pipe maker to sell to a handful of private customers and to sell impersonally through his website, but direct solicitations by phone, email or asking, at a pipe show, "why don't you buy one of my pipes?" is just too much.

That said, what helps me enjoy the hobby is to make a conscious effort to praise and thank the people who have given me so much. For instance, when I was in Copenhagen in October 2006, thinking about how much I missed Bo Nordh, who had died only three months earlier, I relayed to the pipe makers I was with a few comments that Bo had made to me about them.

I told Ulf Noltensmeier and Per Hansen that Bo thought the S. Bang pipe shapes and stains they had created during the past few years were among the most creative he had ever seen. This is the ultimate compliment to a high grade pipe maker. I told Jess Chonowitsch that Bo repeatedly told me that his perfectionism and attention to detail inspired Bo, and that he told me several times he thought Jess was one of the greatest of all time. I told Lars that Bo attributed much of his success to Lars, to the many lengthy phone conversations they had when Bo was starting out and wanted to talk about pipe shapes with someone who inspired him, someone he could look up to, and he always looked up to Lars.

In other words, I was trying to thank these pipe makers for devoting their lives to making the best pipes they could make, pipes that have become a part of my life. Since they all knew and respected Bo so much, I figured that his high opinion of them was the best way to communicate my gratitude to them. My suggestion is that you think of something similar as a way to thank the people who have made your pipe collecting a part of your life.

Prior to traveling to Copenhagen, my wife and I visited several other European cities, and we attended two musical concerts, one featuring Chopin and the other featuring Mozart and Vivaldi. As I listened to this beautiful music, which I find incredibly relaxing, I thought about the commitment, dedication, creativity and passion that went into each composition. And, of course, I thought about pipes (because I'm always thinking about pipes!).

In my mind I compared Bo Nordh to Beethoven, S. Bang to J.S. Bach, Ivarsson to Mozart and Chonowitsch to Chopin. I don't know why I did this, and I'm sure it's silly, but I feel very comfortable with these comparisons.

You might find it interesting to do the same with your favorite pipe brands. There are many more musical composers than pipe makers, so it should be easy to find one who suits your personality. You don't have to limit yourself to classical music either. One of the advantages of music is that there is no "best," just as there is no best in pipes. There are only our favorites. We all have our favorite music, and our favorite pipe makers, and that's how it should be.

I remember once at a Los Angeles Pipe Show, there was a collector who told me at the Saturday night dinner that he had seen a beautiful Ashton bent sandblast that he couldn't stop thinking about. "The pipe cost $175, and that's more than I wanted to spend," he said. "But now I regret not buying it. I will be sick if it was sold. There's just something about that pipe that I love. I don't know why, but I've got to have it!"

The next morning, as I was sipping a cup of hot coffee, he approached me with a big grin on his face. He pulled out the pipe and said, "I got it! I'm just so happy."

His face had the look of a little kid who just gotten the prefect present at his birthday party, and his glow and excitement made me feel warm all over. I remember cheering him on, congratulating him on getting just what he wanted. And I thought, this is what pipe collecting should be -- finding what we like and then relishing the experience.

Pipes have an almost mystical quality about them, very much like great art. Have you ever sat and just studied one of your favorite pipes? Tried to picture the pipe maker working on it? And don't forget photographs. Beautiful photographs of great pipes can be extremely inspiring, such as in Pipes and Tobaccos magazine and in several excellent coffee table books. Greg Pease, Michael Lindner and Neill Archer Roan all take beautiful pictures of pipes.

Great art, including great music and literature, has stood the test of time. It has endured the slings and arrows of critics. It has survived censorship and ridicule, and I believe great pipes will survive prohibition and ridicule.

This is because great art helps us relax and inspires us to continue going forward to meet life's challenges. This is precisely what relaxed, moderate pipe smoking does for me, and I feel eternal gratitude to the people who have made this possible: pipe sellers, collectors, tobacco blenders, show organizers, pipe writers, photographers and everyone else involved in the industry or hobby. But in particular I thank all pipe makers, who are a combination of artists and craftsmen. Their creations today could last for centuries.

When we focus on the positive, when we feel gratitude for everyone who makes this hobby possible, and appreciate our pipes as great art and great smoking instruments -- as a part of who we are -- it is amazing how uplifting, inspiring and exciting our pipe collecting can be.

CHAPTER SEVEN

~~~~~

THE ENDLESS MYSTERIES OF
PIPE TOBACCO

This is one of my favorite tobaccos, but only after it has been aged and slowly dried out as I describe in this chapter.

Most of my writings are about pipes and pipe makers, but this chapter is about tobaccos. I shy away from the subject as a general rule because I am at a loss to describe the nuances of flavor the way other critics can. I simply enjoy the tobaccos I like after I have stored them in the ways that I describe in this article.

The opening is a continuation of the last chapter. It was my response at the time of the controversy over Bo Nordh in late 2006. But thankfully I only devoted a few paragraphs to the issue before discussing the endless mysteries of pipe tobaccos.

* * * * *

Pipe collectors have many different interests, and that continues to make the hobby lively, stimulating and fun.

We have heard a great deal lately from the traditional collectors who are very interested in fills in pipes, who consider undisclosed fills to be the ultimate sin that a pipe maker can commit. That is fine for those collectors, and they are certainly entitled to their strong opinions on the subject. However, I do not share their passion for this issue. As I wrote in my book, "In Search of Pipe Dreams," when it comes to small surface imperfections in the wood, if they can be hidden, then I want them hidden. Of course, large putty fills are unacceptable to almost everyone, including me.

As for Bo Nordh, he was a friend, and it upsets me to see his character and integrity attacked after he can no longer defend himself. Bo was always honest with me, and he said his pipes had flaws but not fills. I believe him, and I have not seen evidence to the contrary. I realize that some collectors have persuaded themselves that specks in the wood are in fact tiny fills and not natural flaws. Since I am not a craftsman, and I did not make the pipes, I cannot say for certain what they are.

We will never know for sure unless someone allows the stain to be sanded off his Bo Nordh pipe. Not likely --

but this should have been done. Before attacking a man's character and integrity, one has a responsibility to make absolutely certain that the facts are correct. Sanding off the stain of a pipe, so that the wood looks like a popsicle stick, will offer indisputable proof as to whether a black dot on the surface is a tiny fill or only a natural flaw. Until then, it is all guesswork, and a matter of trust or distrust of the pipe maker.

All we can do in the meanwhile is to "agree to disagree" about the relative importance, or insignificance, of this subject. As I wrote in my "Ode to Pipe Collecting," I much prefer reading about issues related to pipes and tobaccos that make collectors happy.

We can have spirited intellectual debates about all kinds of exciting topics without making them personal. I love pipes as a temporary escape from the responsibilities of business, family, church, travel, exercise and many other obligations making demands on my time. Pipes help me relax, and I refuse to relinquish my enjoyment of this wonderful hobby by spending time on anything other than that which gives me pleasure, joy and fulfillment.

What interests me most are the friendships that I have made with fellow pipe smokers and pipe collectors, the camaraderie that exists at pipe shows and in conversations, and the yearning that we all have to learn more about the endless mysteries of briar pipes and pipe tobaccos. This is one of the reasons that I am in awe when I see the monumental achievements of great pipe makers as they turn a block of briar into a work of art that is both practical and aesthetically beautiful.

And it is these mysteries that have led me to discover variations in, and experiments with, existing tobacco blends that make their taste unrecognizable from the original, almost as if I have created an entirely new blend without ever meaning to.

Most experienced pipe smokers prefer tins of tobacco to giant bags known as "bulk tobaccos," but one of my all-time favorite blends is the bulk version of Dunhill Early

Morning Pipe.

However, in thinking about it, what I really mean is that one of my all-time favorite blends is Dunhill Early Morning bulk after it has been aged for years, dried out, pulverized, mixed with an aged Early Morning that is still moist (either tinned or bulk), put in a McClelland can and periodically shaken over a period of months.

My discovery of this unusual aging and blending process was mostly by accident, and the end result is a product quite different in taste from the Early Morning that is available at your local tobacconist, either in tins or bulk.

It is so different, in fact, that knowledgeable pipe collectors who are familiar with the original blend simply cannot recognize it.

"There's no way you can convince me that this is Early Morning," said Ed Lehman, as he savored this unique pipe tobacco.

Ed was in my den, otherwise known as my pipe room, on a Friday before the 2002 Los Angeles Pipe Show. He looked in the closet and saw dozens of different pipe tobaccos, mostly English blends with Latakia, all stored in McClelland's special 50-gram and 100-gram tins.

Ed was a Virginia man, but on that day he was in the mood to try something different. He put one of his beautiful Dunhill Red Barks, with a specially-made giant gold band, on my desk and said, "Surprise me. Pick one of the blends that doesn't have too much Latakia, and who knows, maybe I'll like it."

So naturally I thought of Early Morning, which has lots of Oriental as well as Latakia. Without telling Ed which blend I had chosen, I filled up his pipe using my usual method of pouring the tobacco into the bowl.

I mention this because Pipes and Tobaccos magazine recently offered a number of different ways to load your pipe, and I have tried them all and find each one useful, depending on the size of the tobacco chamber and on whether the tobacco is wet or dry, ribbon cut, cube cut and other similar factors.

But since my Early Morning was extremely dry, I used the system for filling tobacco that is my favorite: I put a blank sheet of paper on the desk and held Ed's pipe over it in my left hand. With my right hand, I poured the tobacco into the bowl, shaking the pipe a little and tapping it on the side to let the granules settle. Once the bowl was filled, I tamped down the tobacco with my index finger and then handed the pipe to Ed.

The reason for the blank sheet of paper is that when you pour out the tobacco, a fair amount spills to the side. I'd rather have the spill confined to a single sheet of paper than be spread out all over the desk. When finished, I curl up the paper and pour the tobacco back into the tin.

As Ed gently puffed on his pipe, he would occasionally smell the smoke curling out of his bowl. I told him it was my own version of Dunhill Early Morning.

"No, seriously, what is this blend?" he asked. "I've tried Early Morning off and on for 40 years, and this is totally different. I've tried it as No. 27, and I like this better. What is it? And how can I buy some?"

No. 27 was the hand-blended version of Early Morning that the Dunhill store in London used to sell in 50-gram tins.

I explained that the whole thing came about by accident. In 1994 I bought a 5-pound bag of Early Morning bulk from Bob Hamlin. Bob has been around pipe tobacco for decades, and I always learn from him.

"My advice is to open the bag and make five 1-pound bags out of it," he said. "That way, if any problems develop over time, such as mold or whatever, they won't contaminate all five pounds."

Bob also recommended that I buy one of those machines that seal the plastic bags so they are air tight. I found one at the local Sears store and happily spent a few hours on a Sunday afternoon creating five air-tight 1-pound plastic bags of 1994 Early Morning bulk.

I have read that plastic can leave a smell on the tobacco, so it is important that you use what is known as "food grade plastic," which is the kind found in your local supermarket. Baggies that are made for packing luncheon sandwiches and celery and carrots -- that is the type of plastic to use for packing your tobacco.

Mike McNiel of McClelland Tobacco Company is big on "food grade" everything, and he had all of the McClelland tins lined with what is known as a "food grade coating." Mike got the idea for the special lining from one of his customers, who was an avid pipe smoker and a top executive at a large company that specialized in canned vegetables and was on the cutting edge of new technology in that field.

"We were able to use the molds from the cans they were producing," Mike said.

This makes sense when you consider that tobacco is a vegetable. I remember once at a Chicago Pipe Show seminar when the speaker, Frank Blews of Lane Ltd., told us to be very careful in how we store our tobacco because we are in reality storing a vegetable. And Mike McNiel said tobacco is related to the tomato plant family.

"Yes, I've tried smoking a dried tomato vine, and it was terrible!" Mike said.

So McClelland's solution of using the same canning techniques and linings as a giant vegetable company made the McClelland tins particularly appealing to me. I'm not sure if they are technically known as "tins" or "cans," but I use both terms interchangeably.

I should say that McClelland's tobaccos are among my favorites also, including a blend that they made specially for Barry Levin called Scottish Woods. This blend was available from 1989 until 1994, and then it was discontinued, though McClelland's did make a limited run in 2004 for the Columbus Pipe Show. Mike said recently that many customers have requested that he start making Scottish Woods again, including an entire pipe club, and there is a possibility he will start offering the blend for sale again in the future.

But back in 1994, when I was ordering the Early

Morning bulk from Bob Hamlin, I also ordered my usual six tins of Scottish Woods -- until Bob told me the blend was soon to be discontinued. I panicked ... and decided to order a hundred tins. I have been smoking them ever since, and they keep getting better with age. I still have about 50 left. The tins are the larger 100-gram size, and each time I finished one, I would fill up the empty tin with Early Morning bulk.

I also smoke three other McClelland blends regularly -- the original Frog Morton, Butera's Latakia No. 1 and Tad Gage's 3 Oaks -- and they all come in 50-gram tins. After I finish smoking all the tobacco in the tin, I then use it to store my other tobaccos.

Except for two ceramic tobacco jars – one from David Field and the other a Dunhill My Mixture jar that I bought from Bob Noble -- I like the McClelland's tins so much that I transfer all tobaccos to them, including tins of the Dunhill blends, Balkan Sobranie, Esoterica and all other tobaccos. Whenever I travel to a different city I try to find a pipe store and usually buy two-to-four ounces of one of their house English blends. When I get home, I transfer the tobacco to an empty McClelland tin.

I simply put the plastic top on and leave the tins in my closet. Air does seep through, which I find useful for drying the tobacco slowly. If you prefer a more moist tobacco, Mike McNiel recommends pressing a piece of aluminum foil over the tobacco as a moisture barrier before putting the plastic lid on the can.

To label my tobaccos in the McClelland tins, I use a magic marker on a piece of paper and write down the name of the blend and year and then cut the paper and tape it to the side of the tin. For instance, I have a 100-gram McClelland tin in my closet that says, "DUNHILL EARLY MORNING bulk 1994, 1995, 2000 and tinned 1998."

Now the one that I gave Ed Lehman had only one year on it, 1994. But since then, as my supply dwindled, I mixed a combination of bulk and tins of Early Morning blends from those other years listed on the label. The reason for taping the label on the can is so I can easily note changes in the dating for the tobaccos as I continually refill the cans. Also, if I change tobaccos in the can, I just tear off the old label and put on a new one.

But these are the tins that I have in the closet to use for my daily smoking, as opposed to the tobaccos that I have in storage. The ones in the closet never stay there too long -- rarely more than a year -- so I don't worry about maintaining a constant temperature, which is important for storing tobacco, especially if you plan on "cellaring" it for years and years.

When I first heard about the constant temperature issue, I realized there was no room in my house that stayed at a constant temperature. The heat and cold fluctuated as did the humidity and dryness of the air. For years I simply used a closet and never really addressed the problem. But then one day, quite by accident, I discovered a miraculous solution.

I was in a sporting goods store picking up some weight lifting equipment, and the store was having a sale on picnic coolers. I don't mean the styrofoam type but rather the ice chests that even allow for cooling inside. I have heard that when you store pipe tobacco, if you have a choice between too cold or too hot, always take too cold.

Stacked on top of each other near the cash register, there were dozens of the blue-and-white coolers, all with a shiny white coating inside that guaranteed insulation. I saw immediately that my tobacco could be stored in the coolers at a constant temperature for a period of many years, regardless of the outside room temperature.

I bought two on the spot and have since bought many more. I simply open and close the ice chest tops when I want to put in or take out tobacco. I do not have the fancy kind where you can actually set the temperature inside the cooler. My only goal is a constant temperature, and that is achieved by the nature of the insulation that picnic cooler ice chests provide.

In 1994, with my five 1-pound bags of Early Morning bulk, I opened one of the bags and took out enough to fit into the empty McClelland's 100-gram tin that I had after smoking all of the Scottish Woods that was originally packed into it. I put the tin in my closet and smoked it occasionally as I smoked many other blends.

After six months, when there was only a small amount left, and it was very dry, I noticed a distinct improvement in the taste of the tobacco. It was slightly sweet, which I had never experienced before with Early Morning, and it had a nutty flavor and was incredibly mellow to smoke. I then transferred another four ounces into the same tin and put it back in my closet.

Was it the dryness of the tobacco? Or the unique McClelland can? Or some other variable that affected the taste of the tobacco? I didn't know then, and I don't know now.

After a few more months, I noticed that every bowl had that great taste. I liked it so much that I filled up a second empty Scottish Woods tin and put it on a shelf in the back of the closet. Fortunately, I forgot about that one and continued refilling and smoking the first one.

When I went through my tobaccos a few years later, I found the second tin. I pulled off the plastic top and felt the tobacco, which was seriously dried out at this point. It had lost much of its delicious aroma, but when I smoked a bowl, it smoked even better than before. Smelled worse but smoked better -- why, I'll never know, but this is a phenomenon I have observed many times.

I could not believe how great it tasted! For some reason, I started crumpling the tobacco in my fingers, rubbing it out as if it had been a flake tobacco. I then got a large popcorn bowl and started really rubbing out the tobacco to let it drop into the bowl. This had the same effect as Steve Fallon's blender, where in both cases we are pulverizing our tobacco into tiny granules. I kept rubbing and rubbing until much of the tobacco was smaller than grains of pepper, with dust floating into the air. I poured the four ounces back into the 100-gram tin and realized that it filled less than a third of the tin -- where previously it went to the top. So I opened the picnic cooler with the Early Morning bulk, took out a bag and filled the bottom two-thirds of the McClelland tin with the more moist "stored" tobacco. I poured the pulverized tobacco on top.

Periodically, I would shake the tin, but since it was full it had little effect. So I dumped everything back into the popcorn bowl and mixed the pulverized tobacco with the semi-moist "stored" tobacco and then put it all back into the tin.

It was a very good smoke, but since I only occasionally used that tobacco, it sat in the closet that way for many months. Each time I tried a bowl I noticed that all of the tobacco was a little drier and the taste continued to improve. As I smoked more and more of the tobacco, I just instinctively would shake the McClelland tin before loading a new bowl. Why? Beats me. Did it help? I don't know. All that I know is that it was becoming my favorite tobacco.

By the time Ed was in my den, that Early Morning bulk had been in storage in a picnic cooler for at least seven years and in the McClelland tin for at least six months. Some of it had been pulverized and then mixed with an equal amount of moist ribbon cut of the same blend from the same bag. All of it had been shaken many times. It was crispy on the outside and only slightly moist on the inside. And it was perfect.

Several times over the years I would try to rush the drying process by having the tobacco exposed to the open air for a few days or even weeks, and every time, the results were disappointing. The tobacco lacked all those nuances and special flavors, and the smoke invariably gave me tongue bite. In other words, the old adage, "patience is a virtue," has special meaning when it comes to drying out your pipe tobacco.

Mike McNiel points out that all the aging, drying out and patience in the world won't do a bit of good if the tobacco blends used a green leaf.

"That's why at McClelland we use ripe leaf only for our tobaccos and then try to age them at least seven years before they are sold in our vacuum-packed special cans," he said.

I still use the Sears sealing machine at times, but more often than not, I just use baggies. I have found that the tobaccos taste better if they are put in gallon size baggies or food and storage bags (I always use two for a double lining) and then tightened at the top with a pipe cleaner. Yes, a little air does get into them, but if they are kept in the picnic coolers, you'd be amazed at how moist the tobacco is once you get past that outer layer. By allowing a little air in, however, I find that the blends taste better than if they are hermetically sealed. Why? I have no idea.

I have also noticed that different years with the same blend yield different results. For instance, Early Morning 1994 tastes better to me than Early Morning 1995, though there is only a slight variation. I believe this relates to the fact that tobacco is a vegetable, and some crop yields are more tasty than others.

Because my Early Morning bulk results were so successful, I have bought 2-pound and 5-pound bags of Dunhill 965, Dunhill Nightcap and Lane's Crown Achievement. I also have plenty of old tins of these blends, and I mix the moist tinned tobacco with the dried and pulverized bulk versions of the same tobacco and store them all in the McClelland "food grade" cans. It is amazing how clean these tins look inside even after holding tobacco every day for 13 years.

I hope some of these experiments and suggestions are helpful to you, and I hope you are able to try some for yourself. It's just so much fun to experiment and to find what you like about pipe collecting and pipe smoking. We will never learn the answers to all the mysteries about briar and about tobaccos, but the search for those answers can provide for a lifetime of fun.

CHAPTER EIGHT

~~~~~

BROKEN PIPES

Three of my closest friends in the pipe world have died since I wrote so much about them in my first book, "In Search of Pipe Dreams." I miss all three every day.

Ed Lehman contracted Hepatitis C as a young man, and it finally caught up with him when he was 71 in 2004. Bo Nordh was paralyzed in a motorcycle accident as a teenager, and the doctors marveled that he lived to age 65. Jim Benjamin's heart of gold gave out when he was 84.

I lost other pipe friends during this same period as well, including Gordon Soladar, an attorney who worked his way through law school helping to make the JHW pipes, who passed away in his sleep in 2004; Ed Kolpin, founder of the original Tinder Box, who died at age 97, and the brilliant German pipe maker, Rainer Barbi, who died from cancer in 2011.

At the time of their deaths, I wrote detailed tributes to Ed Lehman, Jim Benjamin and Bo Nordh, and I have decided to reprint them here as Chapter 8, called "Broken Pipes." That is a term that pipe collectors use to describe their pipes that can no longer be used, and their friends who are no longer alive. I have always thought it a very fitting description for those of us who love our pipes, and it would be difficult to find three men who loved their pipes more than Ed, Jim and Bo.

* * * * *

ED LEHMAN, A GENTLE GIANT

The pipe world, and the whole world for that matter, lost a giant of a man when Ed Lehman went to heaven on March 27, 2004. Ed was a devoted husband to his charming wife, Lillian, and an adoring father to his five beautiful children. He also was a gentle and loving grandfather to his 12 fortunate grandchildren. In addition to providing love and guidance, Ed and Lillian created a family environment that encouraged their children to express their individual personalities, and it is amazing how successful each one has become -- all in totally different fields.

Ed also was an accomplished attorney -- one of the best in his field of intellectual property rights. If you asked him a question, he gave you a clear and direct answer. If he did not know the answer, he would never try to fake it. He would say he didn't know but would find out and get back to you -- which he always did.

Ed's private passion was pipe collecting. I say "private" because in his world as a high-powered attorney, dining regularly at the Union League Club, attending functions near his home in Chicago's fashionable North Shore, Ed was too often forced to put his pipe collecting on hold, especially in recent years as the anti-smokers have become intolerably self-righteous. His love of pipes was something he didn't talk about much in those settings, but he always had secret pipe dreams, and he couldn't wait to get home, sit back in his favorite chair, pull out one of his beloved Dunhill Red Barks, load it with some aged Virginia tobacco, light up, put his feet up, and become totally relaxed and at peace with the world.

My own relationship with Ed began more than four decades ago through our families. My parents knew Ed and Lillian because they belonged to the same Catholic parish in Winnetka, Illinois, known as Saints Faith, Hope and Charity. All of the Lehman children, and the Newcombe children, attended "Faith Hope" grade school.

My youngest brother, John, who is now 44, was best friends with Ed Lehman Jr., who is head of his own law firm based in Beijing -- one of the largest and most successful law firms in all of China. (See what I mean about individualist children?) John told me that some of his favorite Saturday nights in high school were spent at the Lehman's house, where Ed Senior would make pizza for a half dozen "starving" teenage boys. "He would flatten the dough and then twirl it in the air for all of us to see," John said. "He'd either be singing 'O Sole Mio' as he cooked, or we'd be discussing old movies. One of his favorite comedians was W.C. Fields, which is no surprise, because they have the same sense of humor. He would tap his knife on the kitchen counter like a drummer and say, smiling, 'Git outta my kitchen! ... Git outta my kitchen!'"

For years John kept prodding me to get to know his friend Ed's father. I had seen the Lehman family for years at Sunday Mass, said hello a hundred times, but never once talked pipes with Ed in those days. "I think Mr. Lehman has more pipes than you do," John told me many times during the 1980s. So finally, about 15 years ago, I called Ed to introduce myself as a pipe collector, and he said, "It's funny -- I was thinking about calling you because it's so rare that two people from this area are fanatical pipe collectors."

We hit it off immediately, and from that day until last

fall, when he told me he was gravely ill (and I did not want to disturb him), we talked at least once or twice every week -- many hours that literally flew by! And of course, all we talked about was pipes! It was amazing how we could disagree on almost everything in terms of personal taste -- Ed liked long pipes while I liked short ones; he liked straight Virginia while I liked blends with Latakia; his passion was high-grade Dunhills while mine was high-grade Danish (I could go on and on) -- yet we were always very close, laughing, swapping stories, comparing ideas, and just having fun like two little boys who are enthusiastic about a shared passion for their toys.

I remember attending the RTDA in Chicago with Ed about 10 years ago. We took the train together from suburban Wilmette to downtown Chicago, and we had a fantastic time all day. Ed was so proud of a beautiful gold-banded Dunhill ring grain billiard that he picked up from Bob Hamlin. He would slide it out of the case, show me the (very tight) ring grains, put it back in the case, and ... glow. He was so happy! The look on his face was one of pure contentment.

After the show we decided to take a taxi to the train station. At that point, neither of us was smoking because we had smoked all day -- and we had been around a thousand other pipe and cigar smokers, so of course our clothes and hair must have smelled of smoke. The cab we got into was absolutely filthy -- the driver looked and smelled like he hadn't bathed in a month. After driving one block, he started sniffing the air very dramatically. He pulled the car to the side of the road, turned around and said, in an incredibly self-righteous tone, "There's no smoking in this cab!"

Ed and I burst out laughing -- it was unbelievably comical! Between our laughter, we somehow managed to convince the man we were not smoking, but when we were on the train we couldn't help but see that our world really had been turned upside down -- where a smelly cab driver would feel moralistic in lecturing the people paying his fare.

Very profoundly, Ed asked me, "Do you realize that if

Winston Churchill and FDR had hailed that taxi, that driver would have felt justified in kicking them onto the street because they smoked? What is happening to the world?"

But despite the serious undertone, Ed's sense of humor dominated his personality. He was wickedly funny. But you had to get to know him, and be intelligent, to realize how truly funny he was, which was a testament to his own brilliance. One of Ed's carpool friends in high school was Bob Newhart, who went on to become the nationally famous TV star and comedian. They each had a dry wit, and between the two of them, I'm sure those car rides were hysterical.

But Ed was never one to try to become the center of attention. In fact, he was the exact opposite. I can't remember meeting anyone who was a better listener. Ed was genuinely concerned about other people. Kindness was at his core. He was always a celebrity at every pipe show he attended -- not in the sense of glitz and glamour -- but he had a quiet charisma that attracted people to him like a magnet. At six feet, four inches tall, Ed gave new meaning to the term "gentle giant." He loved the camaraderie, and his pipe smoking comrades, so to speak, loved being with him.

One time we each made a last-minute decision to attend the New York Pipe Show, and neither of us knew the other would be there. I had flown in from Frankfurt, and Ed from Chicago. When we saw each other at the Friday night reception, we both beamed! And of course we spent the next few hours laughing and telling stories -- again, like two kids who had been sent away to different summer camps who were suddenly reunited. Ed told me he always left pipe shows feeling filled up. He once wrote a very perceptive article for Pipe Friendly magazine talking about why shows were so important to him and so much fun for him -- because of the warmth, friendships, trading, acquiring, selling, investigating new and old products -- and just having a blast!

The world is so much better because he lived, but his absence creates a painful emptiness for everyone who knew him. He was so proud of his children and grandchildren, and he and Lillian were as close as any couple who ever lived.

I consider myself extremely fortunate to have had the privilege of knowing Ed Lehman. I looked up to him in life, and now, feeling this enormous void, I will look up to him in his after-life, where he is with God, in heaven, looking down at us with his perceptive eyes, warm smile and kind face -- just as he did every day in the 71 wonderful years of his life on earth.

JIM BENJAMIN, R.I.P.

It is fitting that Jim Benjamin died on the Fourth of July. He truly was an American original.

Jim had a gruff speaking voice, like someone out of the Old West, and a heart as big as the Pacific Ocean. He knew the history of Los Angeles pipe stores better than anyone else, served his country overseas during World War II, and was a great fan of all pipes but especially American-made pipes.

Jim died of heart failure in 2007 at a San Diego area hospital at about the same time that Dr. Ralph S. Paffenbarger Jr., an epidemiologist at the Stanford University School of Medicine, died of heart failure. Both men were 84, and both had theories about how to live long and happy lives. Paffenbarger was a pioneer researcher in the importance of exercise to carry us happily into old age, while Benjamin believed that moderate pipe smoking was the key to relaxation and stress reduction.

Of course, it is not surprising that in today's political climate, where anything related to tobacco is condemned, the newspapers barely noticed the passing of Jim Benjamin but devoted paragraph after paragraph to Dr. Paffenbarger's life and groundbreaking findings. While I applaud the latter, I want to make up for the former. I want to pay tribute to my friend and mentor, Jim Benjamin, and to thank him for teaching me so much about this exciting hobby.

Like many of us, Jim was attracted to pipes at an early age. But he was also intrigued by how the pipe makers managed to get such a beautiful shine on the wood and by how they made their mouthpieces sparkle. He started experimenting with what would become the passion of a lifetime back in 1939 when he cleaned his first pipe.

There was a 20-year period in his life, ending in the late 1960s, when Jim became addicted to cigarettes. He gave them up by switching back to a pipe, and he said it was the best decision he ever made. Jim smoked two bowls a day after working for endless hours in his garage/workshop in Rancho Bernardo, a suburb of San Diego, where he had buffing wheels set up on counters along the walls, with gallons of alcohol, thousands of pipe cleaners, dozens of jars of pipe stains and myriad other pipe rejuvenation equipment. Jim liked to relax smoking his pipes late in the evening while watching an old movie on television.

I first read about Jim in "The Ultimate Pipe Book" by Richard Carleton Hacker, and I sent him my first pipes to be cleaned more than 15 years ago. I was overwhelmed by the marvelous job he did. It was so much better than any pipe store had ever done. There was simply no comparison. I sent more and then more, and still more, over the months and years ahead.

We would talk on the phone for hours, and I learned so much about the history of pipes, especially Los Angeles area pipe stores. For instance, he told me about the time that John's Pipe Store of downtown L.A. had a "Pipemobile" similar to Oscar Mayer's "Wienermobile," or about the famous movie director George Sidney and his special tobacco blend called (what else?) "George Sidney Special," or about a boxer-turned-tobacconist in Beverly Hills named Kramer who developed a relationship with a pipe-smoking priest named Dempsey, who was seeking something similar to Dunhill's 965, and how they created "Fr. Dempsey's Tobacco." (Incidentally, both are wonderful blends, and you can still get Fr. Dempsey's at Kramers Pipe and Tobacco Shop in Beverly Hills.)

I remember that Jim took pride in the fact that so many of his customers were medical doctors. "They know that pipes help you relax," he said.

I wrote about Jim for Pipe Friendly magazine and then introduced him to Dayton Matlick, publisher of Pipes and Tobaccos magazine, who did a full-length feature profile with beautiful before-and-after pipe pictures. I also included Jim in my book, "In Search of Pipe Dreams," and several longtime collectors, including Erik Hesse and Ken Campbell, wrote glowing tributes of their own for The Pipe Collector. By the time of his death in 2007, Jim had cleaned and restored thousands of old pipes, and he had dozens still on his bench mid-way through the cleaning process -- pipes from collectors worldwide.

One of his closest friends, collector Steve O'Neill, wrote a very touching tribute to Jim for The Pipe Collector. All of these testimonials in pipe journals were sparked by the collectors' genuine appreciation for the way Jim had helped enhance their pipe smoking enjoyment. In other words, we were all so excited about the job that he did, that we wanted to tell the world about it.

On eBay, the phrase, "cleaned and opened by Jim Benjamin," has been used frequently during the past few years as a way of increasing the sales price of an estate pipe. When it came to cleaning pipes, Jim's favorite phrase was, "The dirtier the better."

I remember once sending him 23 old pipes that I had bought from Tom Colwell. I had spent a day at Tom's house in West Nyack, New York, sifting through his collection of thousands of pipes, and it is hard to fathom how dirty many of them were. Tom was a philosophy professor at New York University, and he compiled a directory of pipe makers, called "Who Made that Pipe?", that is invaluable for collectors interested in the history of pipe making. A few of the pipes that I bought from Tom were more than a century old. I also bought many pipes with American brand names, including pipes by W.C. Demuth, L & H Stern, Bertram's, Wally Frank, Marshall Field's, Barclay-Rex, Weber, and Wilke.

They were filthy when I boxed them up before shipping them to Jim, and each one looked BRAND NEW when they were returned. I could see raw wood inside the pipes, the outside stains on the wood were bright and shiny and the mouthpieces sparkled as if they had just been made. He would spend as much as 10 hours cleaning and restoring a single pipe and never charge more than $25. This was clearly a labor of love.

Early one morning a few years ago I got a call from Jim, who was practically breathless. "I've been lying awake nights trying to remember what kind of oil GBD used to polish their pipes," he said. "At 4 o'clock this morning I remembered! I bolted out of bed and ran to the garage to try it, and you can't believe how rich the polish on these pipes now looks!"

Jim told me the name of the oil, and I wish I could remember what it was, but I was much more intrigued by the psychology of the event than I was by the specific polishing compound. I was so impressed by Jim's passion, by his total commitment to experimenting, learning and always trying to do better.

Jim just loved pipes. He loved everything about them. Once he retired from the motion picture business, where he worked for many decades, he devoted his time to pipes -- pipes sent to him by collectors from all over the world -- pipes that arrived used, worn, tired and dirty, sometimes filthy -- pipes that were sent back clean, polished, shiny and looking brand new. He enhanced the smoking and collecting enjoyment of thousands of pipe smokers, and he will be missed greatly. Pipe collecting just won't be the same without Jim Benjamin.

A TRIBUTE TO BO NORDH

Bo Nordh gave new meaning to the concept of making lemonade out of a lemon. Faced with being a paraplegic as a teenager after a motorcycle accident, he could have spent a lifetime feeling sorry for himself, cursing his fate that life had been so unfair to him. But instead, Bo reached for the stars, and as a pipe maker, he managed to touch a few. Bo's commitment to excellence was unsurpassed. He created some of the most interesting shapes in the history of pipe making. They were also some of the most copied.

Bo's pipes are unquestionably among the greatest smokers ever made, and he never lost sight of the fact that he made pipes to be used and not just displayed for their beauty. Bo spent hours and hours on the smallest detail. He also spent years mulling over possible new shapes before he settled on one.

If the marketplace is the measure, then Bo, without a doubt, was the most successful pipe maker in history. Who else has seen one of his pipes sell for more than $30,000? Just the thought of such a price tag was unfathomable a generation ago. But Bo never cared about money. In fact, he usually described himself as "a poor man who can't even afford to smoke my own pipes unless they have flaws in them."

Bo loved nature. One of his most popular shapes was the snail, and in his studio he displayed a picture of a snail alongside his snail-shaped pipe. Many of us who visited Bo's house near Malmo have sat outside with him, smelling the neighboring wheat fields, or watching Bo as he carefully examined the roses in his garden.

During the 2006 pipe show in Chicago, two months before his death, I ate lunch with Bo almost every day, and I was always impressed by the way he paid attention to small details. For instance, at our first meeting, on the day before the show started, I had lunch with Bo and the man who truly had become his best friend in the pipe world, Per Bilhall, along with Bonnie and Jess Chonowitsch, Chicago collector Vic Griseta and Sykes Wilford of smokingpipes.com.

We had lunch at Pizzeria Due's, which is one of Chicago's world famous deep-dish pizza restaurants. Politicians, celebrities, athletes and ordinary people from all over the world pay homage to Due's when they are in Chicago. I sat next to Bo and was curious to hear what he thought of the pizza. Now with Bo, everything was concentration. Once he started studying something, he gave it his full attention. He chewed for a few minutes, looked up and smiled and said, "The sausage is better than the cheese. Now I know why Chicago is famous for its sausage. The cheese is mozzarella from a cow when it should be from a buffalo. But it's still pretty good!"

When we had lunch at the Pheasant Run Resort during the Saturday and Sunday of the pipe show, Bo always ordered French onion soup, and he savored each spoonful. Then we would go outside, where the air was clear and crisp and the weather was beautiful both days.

"Listen," he said, cupping his right ear with his right hand.

"I can't hear anything," I said.

"Shhh! Just be patient."

I kept listening but couldn't hear anything, and then all of a sudden, I realized that a little bird was chirping.

"Isn't that beautiful?!" Bo asked, with a big grin on his face.

The next day something similar happened, only this time it involved the first green buds on a tree that I failed to notice until Bo pointed them out to me. They really were beautiful.

"I love the springtime," Bo said. "It's the start of something new -- a new beginning."

Bo also loved music -- classical music and rock-and-roll, but his all-time favorite was jazz. Bo bought hundreds of CDs when he and Per toured Chicago in the days before the pipe show. During the actual show, Bo did several things that revealed he had no idea that he had cancer. First, he ordered a three-year subscription to Pipes & Tobaccos magazine. And second, when he found a certain type of aged Virginia tobacco that he liked, he bought enough to last him many years.

I do remember at one point when we were having lunch, Bo looked at me with that wry smile of his and said, "Can you believe that I'm 65? I feel very lucky."

Bo took pride in exercising and keeping himself as fit as possible, given the confines of the wheelchair. He always wanted to get around on his own power and only asked for a push if it was absolutely necessary, such as on a very steep incline.

When Bo gave a lecture, accompanied by a slide show with photographs of his beautiful pipes over the years, I sat in the audience between Lars Ivarsson and Jess Chonowitsch, two of Bo's closest pipe-making friends. They both were impressed by Bo's extraordinary progress as a pipe maker over the years and by his achievement of excellence during the course of his lifetime.

At the same time, Bo always kept his sense of humor, which was totally contagious. Bo could make anyone laugh, and that's what I remember most about him -- laughing alongside Bo. Once he discovered the Internet, he became unstoppable! Bo loved reading and then forwarding jokes. When he discovered these Internet jokes, he always reminded me of a big kid who had committed a minor infraction and was sneaking around the house, hoping his parents wouldn't catch him.

Bo told me his all-time favorite joke on the Internet was a cartoon showing an elderly woman on an elevator. A beautiful younger woman gets on, and the elderly woman sniffs perfume in the air.

"Romance by Ralph Lauren," says the younger woman with a haughty air as the elevator doors close. "$150 an ounce."

A few floors later the elevator stops again and another well-dressed young lady gets on, with the same routine of the elderly woman sniffing the air and the younger woman, as condescendingly as possible, saying: "Chanel No. 5. $200 an ounce."

A few more floors and the elevator stops. As the elderly woman is about to get off, she farts loudly and says, "Broccoli ... 49 cents a pound."

Bo just howled and howled!

I think he liked those types of harmless jokes because their humor provided a great release from the stress he placed on himself to come as close to perfection as possible in his pipe making. He had intensely loyal customers in Europe, America and Africa, as well as in China, Japan, and Russia -- all over the world -- and they always expected the very best, because Bo had spoiled them over the years with his fantastic creations. He also raised the bar for every pipe maker in the world.

In the end, what we will remember most is that Bo Nordh achieved greatness in his lifetime, and he made all of us so much richer because he lived.

CHAPTER NINE

WHAT MAKES A GOOD SMOKING PIPE?

Mark Twain said the most important factor in describing a good smoking pipe is whether you like it -- that's all that counts.

Nothing could be more basic than asking the simple question, "what makes a good smoking pipe?", yet nothing could be more complex than trying to answer it. I tried to do just that in a speech at the banquet dinner of the Los Angeles Pipe Show in 2005. This generated an enormous amount of discussion and interest, and, while there was no consensus, I particularly liked the assertion made by a pipe store manager that, in the end, "the experience" makes for a good smoking pipe more than anything else.

* * * * *

During the holiday season between Christmas and New Year's, our family went skiing in Canada, and our son, Jack, who was 22 at the time, asked me a question that every pipe smoker has asked at one time or another, and probably many times over, a question that has persisted through hundreds of years of pipe smoking: What makes a good smoking pipe?

Now Jack does not actually smoke a pipe. He enjoys an occasional cigar, and he had asked a few of his twenty-something friends if they felt like getting together at a cigar lounge after dinner. They all said yes, except one of the young men, Dean Tallant, said he preferred a pipe.

"A pipe?! You've got to meet my dad!" Jack said. "He loves pipes. He's fanatical about them."

I heard about this conversation an hour later, when I met Jack in the hotel room, and he enthusiastically told me that Dean is a pipe smoker.

"Oh, by the way," Jack said, innocently. "Dean wants to know what makes a good smoking pipe. I'm sort of in a hurry, so can you tell me in a just a sentence or two?"

I wish I knew, I said. I'll be happy to talk to Dean about it, but it is an extremely complicated subject, and there are many diverse opinions. Ask a dozen pipe smokers, and you'll get 20 different answers.

The brilliant Albert Mendez refers to a Latin maxim from Medieval times, "De Gustibus Et Coloribus Non

Disputandum," which means, there is no arguing about tastes and colors.

Define yellow. What makes red pretty? Why does that person dislike green, while this person loves it? Which tastes better, vanilla or chocolate ice cream?

To some extent, when it comes to pipes, our evaluations are no more sophisticated or objective than the answers to those questions. In other words, it all depends on what you like.

But is this a totally subjective field, where arbitrary whim replaces rational analysis and objective criteria? I don't think so.

The crux of rationality, however, is to be able to distinguish between the objective and the subjective, between reality and fantasy.

We must acknowledge that when it comes to pipes, there are plenty of areas that fall into the category of "objective reality." How much a pipe weighs is not a matter of opinion. Its weight is a fact of reality. Whether a pipe is drilled dead center or a little to the left, or a little to the right, is a matter of fact, not opinion. The diameter of the tobacco chamber can be measured objectively. The drilling for the area where the smoke hole enters the tobacco chamber -- is it high, low, or just where it is supposed to be?

We can objectively measure the size, height, and length of the pipe bowl, and the thickness of the wood. The same for the mouthpiece.

The point is -- there are clearly demonstrable objective facts about how a pipe is made.

Are we then to conclude that a good pipe is indeed a matter of objective fact? Can we say that there are experienced pipe smokers who know better than others how to evaluate the smoking qualities of a pipe, precisely because they know how a pipe should be drilled while the beginners do not?

I'm sure there are pipe smokers who believe this to be true, but I am not one of them. I'm sure there are pipe makers, both individuals and factories, who believe this to be true, who believe that their pipes always smoke better than other pipes, but I am not convinced that what they offer is anything more than their own very unscientific experience.

So what are some of the obvious factors that influence our evaluation of whether a pipe is a good smoker?

Well, the shape and size of the pipe are obviously important. When we visit a tobacconist or look over a table full of pipes at a pipe show, the first thing that jumps out at us is the shape of the pipe and its size. Do we like the way it looks? And can we see ourselves smoking it?

Of course, the stain plays just as important a role in our initial examination as well. Does the color of the pipe appeal to us? My friend Ed Lehman loved red colored pipes, especially with gold bands, but the Internet pipe maestro Rob Cooper, another friend, told me that pipes with an orange stain sell better than pipes with red stains. I'm sure Ed was told that, and I'm sure he said, "so what." We pipe smokers know what we like, for us, for our individual tastes, and that is all that counts.

The same with the grain on the pipe bowl. Some people are fanatical about straight-grained pipes, while other people could not care less. They only care about whether the pipe is a good smoker. But our lovers of straight-grained pipes would say that they cannot enjoy a pipe with bald spots or even a cross grain. Personally, my favorite grain is bird's eye that is so dense that it looks three dimensional, but I know there are plenty of pipe collectors who disagree with me and prefer the straight-grains.

Either way, I believe that our perception of the stain and grain influence our evaluation of the smoking qualities of a pipe.

The same for the mouthpiece. I prefer narrow and thin vulcanite, but other people prefer wide and think lucite. It helps to know what you like, which usually comes from experience. The length of the mouthpiece is also a factor that influences our evaluation of a pipe.

Of course, how we acquire a pipe affects our

assessment of whether we think it is a good smoker. If your wife special-ordered a pipe in your favorite shape as a birthday present, you might treasure that pipe as your favorite -- and that can influence your belief that it is a great smoker.

Do you prefer bent or straight pipes? Or maybe the partially bent ones? These too influence whether or not we like a pipe.

Then there is the extremely important issue of brand. Who made the pipe, and what has been your experience with this brand of pipes? I try to give any brand of pipe a second chance. If I buy a pipe and it is a bad smoker, I'm willing to try it once more, but if I get two bad smokers in a row, that's it. I won't go near that brand again.

The reverse is true, too. When I find a great smoker, I will buy a second, a third, a fourth and who knows how many of that brand of pipe.

A good illustration from my personal experience involves the great Italian pipe maker, Paolo Becker. Twenty years ago I fell in love with the aesthetics of Becker pipes, when I saw photos of them on the back covers of the old Pipe Smoker magazine. I could not afford them at the time.

But seven years later, in 1992, I bought my first Becker pipe from Barry Levin. It was a used bent bulldog. I remember being so excited when I opened the box, pulled out the pipe, which had been reamed and cleaned by Jim Cooke, and admired its stunning beauty. I filled it with my favorite tobacco, lit the pipe and settled back, expecting to enjoy the smoke of a lifetime.

And did I? Well, no, not exactly. It was OK. Not bad. Nothing to complain about, and compared with most pipes, it was pretty good. But compared with the favorite pipes in my collection, it was nothing special.

So did I then get rid of it and write off Paolo Becker? No. His pipes were too pretty not to give them a second chance. I bought a second Becker pipe -- a silver-banded, unsmoked free hand with a large bowl and a vulcanite mouthpiece. And the result? Ahh ... just what I had imagined for all those years. It was a fantastic smoker from the very first bowl, and it has only improved with age.

Then I bought a third Becker pipe, a slightly bent free hand apple with a thin vulcanite mouthpiece. The result? Pure heaven. The pipe smokes like a dream.

So now I know that when I see Becker pipes, they are worth examining very carefully. The brand name "Becker" has significant meaning for me.

But why didn't that first pipe measure up to the next two? Here are some possible explanations, and they all help explain what makes a pipe a great smoker:

First, the good smoking pipes were new, not used. Was the first pipe not cleaned out properly? That is possible. Now you should know that I regard Jim Cooke as one of the best pipe makers of all time, and his sandblasts are simply the best in the world, according to many experts.

But making a pipe and cleaning a used pipe are totally different processes, and Jim has told me that he was under tremendous pressure to clean thousands of pipes for Barry each year. I have no doubt that if Jim Cooke could have spent half a day cleaning and restoring the Becker pipe, it would have been a much improved smoke.

So returning to our question (what makes a good smoking pipe?), we can see that how clean the pipe is can make an enormous difference in determining whether we think it is a good smoker. Pretend that a pipe were totally filthy, with left-over marks on the mouthpiece from someone else's saliva ... it could be a $10,000 pipe and I don't think any of us would want to touch it.

What about the briar? Since briar is a part of nature, part of a living organism before it is turned into a pipe, then obviously it can be unpredictable. Some briar smokes better than other briar. Maybe that's why two of my Becker pipes smoked so much better than the first one.

You should know that there are experienced pipe smokers, and pipe makers, who believe that the briar is the most important factor in determining whether a pipe becomes a fantastic smoker. Fred Hanna, a psychology professor and a pipe smoker for more than 30 years, has originated what he calls the "brand-myth thesis." Tom Eltang, a highly respected pipe maker from Denmark, agrees with Fred, as does Regis McAfferty, a novelist who writes extensively about pipes. Many other knowledgeable collectors also agree.

Their basic assumption is that inexpensive but well made factory pipes can smoke the same as high grade, hand made, beautifully crafted pipes that sell for thousands of dollars. If 50 pipes are all made the same way, and some smoke better than others, then clearly the differences in briar account for the differences in smoking quality. You've got to admit, they have a point.

But hold on, said the late Sixten Ivarsson, universally recognized as one of the greatest pipe makers of all time. The flaw in their theory is the assumption that 50 pipes are all made the same way. There is a great difference in the way pipes are made.

Sixten said the creation of a great smoking pipe was "ninety percent physics, five percent materials and five percent magic."

Who is right on this point? The ones who say briar or the ones who say physics? I don't know, and I don't think we will ever know for sure. But we do know for sure that there are exceptions to nearly every rule, and that we can find an occasional lemon from the most expensive brand and an occasional gem from the least expensive brand.

At this point, I know there are some pipe smokers who are ready to throw up their hands in frustration. "Stop with all this analysis and just enjoy your pipes!" they say. They would rather be fat, dumb and happy than spend even a nanosecond fretting over what makes one pipe smoke better than another pipe.

And they too have a point. We can take the pleasure out of pleasure by over-analyzing it. That is why I am totally opposed to a blind taste test for pipes. Pipe smoking should be a relaxing, pleasurable experience enjoyed among friends or in a quiet place alone, but it was never intended to be part of a clinical trial for white coated scientists in a laboratory.

That is why I am trying to focus on the areas that influence the smoking qualities of a pipe that we can understand, and in some cases control, with the goal being to enjoy our pipes even more.

So what are some other factors that affect the smoking quality of a pipe?

One is the opening of the draft hole and the air channel through the mouthpiece. Jim Benjamin, who has been restoring pipes for decades, believes the opening and cleanliness of the pipe are at the top of the list, and I am inclined to agree with him.

Another factor affecting our enjoyment of a pipe is our experience as pipe smokers. The longer we smoke, the more we know what we like.

Another contributing component is the surrounding environment. Sitting poolside under the blazing sun in 120° heat in Palm Springs in August will make it difficult to enjoy any pipe, while just about every pipe will smoke well if it is snowing outside and you are curled up in a comfortable chair by the fireplace enjoying a good book.

Along the same lines, our moods affect the smoking quality of our pipes. In a good mood, a pipe can smoke like a dream, while in a bad mood, the same pipe, with the same tobacco, can be totally unsatisfying.

Nearly all of the pipes that I have owned became better each time I smoked them. The more broken-in a pipe is, the better it smokes. Sometimes this process can take years and years -- when all of a sudden a pipe goes from good to great.

But Shane Pappas, a retired pipe store owner who was active in organizing the Los Angeles Pipe Show for many years, said the opposite. "The best smoke from a pipe is always the very first bowl," Shane said. "It only gets worse with each successive bowl." There are times when I agree with Shane too, when I am at a pipe show and maybe have just bought two new pipes and light them up almost immediately -- and just savor the experience!

You might be tempted to ask, who's right on this point -- Shane saying a new pipe or old-time collectors saying a broken-in pipe? I'll answer that question with a question: which is better, chocolate or vanilla ice cream?

Our senses of sight, touch, taste and smell all affect our evaluation of whether a pipe is a good smoker. And that takes us full circle to where we started, i.e., there is no arguing about tastes and colors.

Of course, there are the objective facts that help us determine whether or not a pipe is well made. And we all have legitimate reasons for the choices we make. In other words, a rational process governs.

But in the end, we cannot answer the question, "what makes a good smoking pipe?" in any definitive way. We are all influenced by countless external and internal factors that help us decide whether a pipe is a good smoker.

Whatever pipes you choose as your favorites, they are your favorites. To paraphrase Mark Twain, the only standard governing tobacco is the choice the tobacco lover makes for himself. So enjoy your favorite pipes with your favorite tobacco, knowing that, however you decide to approach this unique hobby of pipe collecting, you have made the correct decision, and whatever pipes you choose as your favorites, you have made the right choice.

CHAPTER TEN

~~~~~

PIPE PRICES AND PIPE FRIENDSHIPS

Jeff Gracik of J. Alan Pipes made this beauty at my request, which was his interpretation of a Lars Ivarsson design. Jeff's pipe looks beautiful and smokes like a dream.

As the prices of pipes continued to climb over the years, I found myself feeling increasingly uncomfortable, and I wanted to address the issue, which is why I wrote this article in January 2011. The hobby appeared to have changed completely, where pipe shows no longer consisted of a bunch of guys trading pipes, similar to baseball card shows, but instead were dominated by table after table of professional sellers with beautiful advertising and photography, and prices that might give pause even to the financiers of Wall Street.

But then it occurred to me, as I thought about my desire to continue attending pipe shows: It's not really about the pipes -- it is about the pipe friendships. That is what makes the hobby so special.

* * * * *

There are so many beautiful pipes being made today that it is breathtaking. The same is true for their prices. But in the end, beautiful pipes pale in comparison to pipe friendships.

I see these two topics as interrelated because of my relentless pursuit of beautiful pipes over a period of decades, while knowing that however much I might admire a certain pipe, the good feelings that come from the camaraderie of pipe collecting are simply invaluable -- they are worth much more than any particular pipe or pipe collection.

It's just like the credit card commercial that puts a price on two or three material objects and then uses the word "priceless" to describe good feelings.

We have seen a sea change in the marketplace for pipes, yet there is no change whatsoever when it comes to the importance of pipe friendships. The camaraderie that we feel at pipe shows was always special, and it remains so. But when it comes to the change in prices, the increases have been jarring. I vividly remember looking at a beautiful

Charatan Crown Achievement with Gordon Soladar at a Los Angeles pipe show many years ago, and the price was $800. "I would never pay that kind of money for a pipe," Gordon said, and I agreed with him.

That was then. Now ... I have heard stories of two different Bo Nordh pipes selling for more than $30,000 each, and I have seen old beat-up, well-smoked Bo Nordh classically-shaped pipes routinely selling for $6,000 and more.

I recently went on the Internet looking for pipes made by Lars Ivarsson, and I could find only three, one for $7,000 and two others for $10,000 each.

This is out of my league. The irony is that I feel partly responsible for this run-up in prices.

I wrote enthusiastically about high-grade Danish pipes throughout the 1990s, and many collectors started buying them. But at the time, collectors like Ron Colter and I would trade with each other and buy and sell used Ivarsson pipes for between $300 and $600. In the early days, you could get a great unsmoked Bo Nordh or Lars Ivarsson pipe for between $1,000 and $2,000. Bo once sold me a sandblast for $300, and I remember buying a used Bo Nordh sandblast from Peter Heinrichs for $700, which I subsequently sold for $1,000. I'm sure that today that same pipe would sell for $5,000 or more.

What happened?

Globalization, free trade and the Internet all came together at the same time. Many professional sellers specialized in high-grade pipes and kept raising their prices, and collectors kept buying them. It did not help that my book, "In Search of Pipe Dreams," was published in 2003, shortly before the initial increase in prices. I wrote about $1,000 pipes, and within a few years, those same pipes were selling for $2,500. But how did they then become $10,000 pipes?

I have asked a number of high-grade pipe sellers, and the answer appears to be China. The Chinese are suddenly willing to pay $10,000, so naturally the sellers and pipe makers are pleased to oblige. The fact that this has occurred only a few years after my book was published in Chinese, with beautiful color photographs in a hard-cover coffee-table format, forces me to ask, "What have I done?" My wife says, "You've created a monster."

This was never my intent, nor do I know who is paying these prices. Of course, I don't mean to imply that I am solely responsible for the astronomical prices of certain high-grade pipes, but I am convinced that, unintentionally, I have contributed to them and priced myself out of the market. Talk about unintended consequences!

There are any number of sellers who specialize in high-grade pipes, and they all use the Internet and, thus, have a worldwide customer base. Also, the pipes in question -- Nordh and Ivarsson -- have become extremely rare, especially compared with what was available when I started writing about them.

But it is not just Nordh and Ivarsson. When I attend a pipe show these days, there are dozens of pipe makers -- genuine artisans -- who routinely charge what would have been considered outrageous prices for their pipes, and they appear to be selling them. There are many customers willing to pay big bucks to add to their collections. In fact, many collectors who joined the hobby in the past five years assume they need to spend a great deal of money to have a decent pipe collection.

This is not necessarily true, and I am concerned that this "sticker shock" (a phrase used by several collector friends when the prices went from $1,000 to $2,500) makes the hobby less fun.

Pipe collecting should not be a rich man's hobby.

It should be open to everyone, and we should encourage all collectors in their choices.

Before his death last year, Bruce Rogers was a member of the Los Angeles Pipe Club, and he was a true character with a warm and generous heart. While in his seventies, Bruce rode his motorcycle to the monthly meetings. He lived in a trailer and made do with his monthly

Social Security check, yet he had a fabulous collection of pipes. He specialized in finding used Stanwells in the $30 range, and every time I saw him, I could have sworn that he was smoking an Ivarsson! That's because he just had a knack for selecting Stanwell pipes that were based on models that Sixten Ivarsson created for the company.

I have many pipes that I purchased for less than $300 that are nice looking and great smokers. Actually, some were made by Ivarsson, S. Bang and Jess Chonowitsch -- pipes that I bought used after spending a great deal of fun time searching for them. Remember, the search should be as much fun as the acquisition. However, it has been at least seven years since I have found one of these bargains.

In other cases, they were used pipes made many decades ago that have been totally cleaned up -- old Dunhills, Sasienis, Comoys, Barlings, Charatans and others -- and there is something special about the old wood and soft rubber mouthpieces. I savor these pipes, and if I were forced to give up my collection and could only keep a dozen of the pipes that I bought for less than $300, I would be fine. But picture giving up your pipe friendships. That would be unimaginable.

This does not mean I don't admire beautiful new pipes. I do admire them. They are like eye candy. At times I even lust after them. I just wish they weren't so expensive.

The situation reminds me of the advice that Vince Gironda, a Hollywood gym owner and trainer of the stars many years ago, gave about weight training. Vince wished out loud that the poundages could be sanded off all the barbells and dumbbells, so no one would know how much they were lifting. That way, they would concentrate 100 percent on good form.

Along the same lines, I would love it if there were no price tags on pipes, and we could evaluate all pipes for their beauty, comfort and smoking qualities, not knowing anything about whether they were considered high grade or low, just our own independent evaluation of the pipe. If that were the case, I believe many more pipe smokers would rave about Ivarssons and Nordhs from firsthand experience.

Since it is impossible to take economics out of the equation, however, what are our alternatives for finding fun and satisfaction in the hobby? The answer is pipe friendships.

You can still put together a fantastic collection of pipes for less than $300 each by searching the Internet, going to pipe shows and making a game out of your quest. But what helps even more is to cultivate friendships in the hobby, so that people routinely alert you to pipes in your area of interest.

Having pipe friends from around the world, people we get together with at pipe shows or through occasional in-person visits, people we stay in touch with by phone and on the Internet, that is what makes the hobby continually exciting.

If you stick around long enough, you will see plenty of people come and go -- they die or lose interest in collecting or decide to quit smoking, or whatever. But an amazing number of collectors remain excited about their pipe collections after years and years of experimentation.

My favorite friends are the ones who stay enthusiastic about the hobby, who always want to learn new things.

This is true of pipe-maker friends, too. Take Bo Nordh, for example. Bo always wanted to experiment. At his last pipe show, in Chicago in May 2006, less than three months before he died, he had asked me to bring him bottles of different types of red stains because he wanted to experiment in developing a signature red stain for his sandblasts.

That desire to learn is typical of many pipe collectors. Rich Esserman, Dave Melnick and I (and many others) were fortunate to know Ed Lehman well, and Ed always had an open mind about trying new things. His excitement and enthusiasm were contagious.

Tom Colwell was the same way. He just loved pipes, tobaccos and everything to do with them.

Tad Gage and Fred Heim have been passionate

collectors for a very long time. I remember one night having dinner with them at a great steakhouse in Indianapolis, where we did not have a reservation and were seated in the kitchen; well, not quite in the kitchen, but almost. We didn't care because we were having fun at an Indiana Briar Friars show! Today, nearly two decades later, all three of us have the same passion for pipes. The fact that we have different specialties (Tad loves Barlings, Fred is Mr. Calabash and I love high-grade Danish) is totally irrelevant.

Who is more devoted to learning than Jim Cooke? He has revolutionized the way pipes are sandblasted because of his tireless dedication over a period of many years, which has always been a labor of love for him.

When Jess Chonowitsch stayed at my house in Los Angeles, I must have asked him a million questions about pipe making, and rather than growing impatient, you could see how animated and excited he got when discussing his craft.

I think one of the reasons pipe friendships become so enduring is because there are so few of us. It is as if we share a secret that no one else knows about. Even the collectors who get into heated arguments frequently smoke a peace pipe together after the dust settles.

In my own case, I have been described in The Pipe Collector as a gullible collector who was so bamboozled that I became a propagandist for high-grade pipe makers, yet I consider these critics to be my friends. Of course, I disagree with them, but these disagreements are really quite minor compared with the big-picture common interest we have in loving our pipes. In many ways, it's us against the world.

Nearly all the great pipe makers became great because of their love of pipe making. They did not do it for the money. In fact, there were times when some of them struggled to make ends meet, but they persisted in following their dream. It is possible that with so many new pipe makers on the scene, some of them are in it for the money, but they won't last.

As for the current high prices, I have mixed feelings.

As a friend of some of the pipe makers, I love the fact that they are earning more money. Also, if a few billionaires ever discover the fun of pipe collecting, then it is possible that someday we will see the first million-dollar pipe sale. Who knows? When it comes to pricing great art, anything is possible.

Yet that raises the question of whether we are talking about great art, to be displayed and admired, or smoking pipes, which are used, banged around and otherwise function as a practical smoking instrument. During the last few years there has been a new breed of collector whose goal is to acquire pipes as works of art, and I admire their pursuit of excellence and recognition of the greatness of certain pipe makers. But the problem is that their deep pockets have driven up the prices of all artisan pipes.

If the prices keep going up, then it becomes a different hobby, and, I believe, a lot less fun.

One solution I have found is to work with relatively new pipe makers who have extraordinary talent. My favorite of those is Jeff Gracik, who makes the J. Alan Pipes. Jeff has made his interpretation of certain pipe masterpieces, and the results are astounding. Instead of paying $15,000 for a smooth Bo Nordh tomato, you can pay $500 for a sandblasted J. Alan Swedish tomato, which is a shape that was inspired by Bo's tomato. What is really interesting, however, is how Jeff has modified the shape so that his version is now uniquely a J. Alan shape. Jeff's pipe smokes unbelievably well. I won't say it is better than Bo's, but I will say it is hard to imagine a better smoker than Jeff's Swedish tomato, which reflects the fact that he spent as much time studying the INSIDE physics of Bo's pipe as he did the outside shape.

There is a shape that Lars Ivarsson created years ago, and I had been looking for one for a long time. It is basically a smooth round ball with a dark sandblasted shank. I kept hoping Lars would make a new version or I would find one on the estate market, but after more than five years of waiting, I decided to ask Jeff to make his version of the pipe. The result was astounding! Even Lars was impressed, and he is not easily impressed. Jeff charged me $800 for the pipe, and it is a fantastic smoker. Had the pipe been made by Lars, the price could easily have cost anywhere from three to 10 times that amount.

So that is a good solution, finding a talented newer pipe maker who can make his own version of a classic masterpiece. Other examples include Lasse Skovgaard's interpretation of a Sixten Ivarsson shape, Alex Florov's version of a Ramses or Peter Heeschen's interpretation of a snail. There are plenty of other examples of excellent pipe makers who are able to capture their own interpretations of masterpiece shapes designed in years past. They are not cheap, but compared with the originals, they are certainly a bargain.

I also want to point out that all of these pipe makers have their own styles and shapes. They only occasionally create their interpretations of certain masterpieces.

There is also the even more important issue, in my opinion, of the internal workings of the pipe, not the outside shape but the inside mechanics. I bought a gorgeous straight-grain freehand from Brad Pohlmann at the West Coast Pipe Show. I love Brad's pipes, but this one did not smoke as well as the others. I looked in my collection and found two Ivarsson pipes that had shapes similar to Brad's -- at least the bend of the shank and mouthpiece was the same. One was made by Sixten in 1962, and the other by Lars in 1984. I sent both pipes to Brad along with his own pipe so he could study them to determine why the two Ivarssons smoked better than his original.

While mediocre pipe makers would have gotten defensive or been offended by my action, Brad's reaction was the opposite: He thanked me for sending the Ivarsson pipes. Brad's desire for excellence makes him one of my new favorites. He spent many hours studying the three pipes, and he told me he saw what was different. He followed the Ivarssons' engineering and sent the pipes back to me, and now his pipe smokes a million times better.

I mention these artisans, Jeff Gracik and Brad Pohlmann, because they are totally committed to being the best pipe makers they can be. The fact that you can get one of their sandblasts for less than $500 is one of the best bargains out there. Buying their pipes now could be like buying Chonowitsches and Bangs 15 years ago.

But if even those prices sound too high, remember Bruce Rogers. His outside limit was $30 for a pipe, and he had one of the best collections I have ever seen.

I figure I'm lucky in that I have bought many great pipes over the years and am in a position to enjoy what I have without ever having to buy another pipe. Of course, I will buy more because I love new pipes. But I believe most experienced collectors feel the same way I do, where they are content with their collection but always open to making a new purchase.

When I attend a pipe show today, it is because of the friendships more than anything else. Buying new pipes is fun, but secondary. I love spending time with like-minded folks who are willing to stand apart from society in pursuing the love of, and the fellowship of, the briar. Our pipe collections are very valuable, but our pipe friendships are priceless.

CHAPTER ELEVEN

~~~~

BALANCE

With my grandson, Scott, on his first birthday.

In between two chapters that discuss money and pipes at some length, I wanted to change the subject a little by telling you about my overall philosophy of life, which includes weaving in pipe collecting as a hobby as opposed to allowing it to consume my life. Many readers have expressed concern about losing themselves in the world of pipes, and others have actually lost themselves without realizing it.

When I was growing up, I remember my father constantly saying, "everything in moderation." It was one of his favorite phrases, and when I was younger, especially as an adolescent, I objected. I was always a wise guy, and I'd say something silly like, "What about a moderate amount of heroin?"

Now that I am older and hopefully a little wiser, I see the importance of moderation as being No. 1 so that my life has balance and each activity -- each area of interest -- is always exciting. If you don't keep some restraints on your love of pipes, you run the risk of burn-out or cynicism, and we have all seen collectors who have changed from an attitude of enthusiasm and excitement to one of extreme negativity.

One of the questions I am asked most often is, "How do you stay so excited about pipes for so long?" and I believe the answer lies in disciplining myself to make sure that this hobby is only one part -- albeit an important part -- of a life filled with goals, love, exercise, creativity and intellectual curiosity.

* * * * *

Nothing is more important to me than living a fulfilled, happy and balanced life. Pipe collecting and pipe smoking are hobbies that I embrace to make my life richer and more enjoyable, but they are not an end in themselves. Many of us who get swept up in the hobby of pipe collecting lose perspective in our pursuit of new acquisitions, rather than using this area of interest as an enjoyable hobby to round out an otherwise productive and love-filled life.

I believe balance is very important in all areas, and I speak as one who is naturally enthusiastic and passionate about my interests, where it would be easy for me to get carried away and lose perspective. For instance, when it comes to business, you have no idea how much I love Creators, the company that I founded in 1987 and have devoted the majority of my waking hours to over the past quarter-century. It is a company that my son, Jack, is now running as president. I always envisioned a successful family business, and the fact that we are doing better under Jack's leadership than at any time in our history is the realization of one of the most important goals of my life. (In case you are interested, our website is www.creators.com.)

Carole and I started dating in 1969 and were married in 1975. We are very close, we complement each other, we try to support our different areas of interest, and, for the most part, we compromise so that each of us gets what we want but never at the expense of the other. You can see examples of this throughout my pipe writings, where we will pick a city that has both -- a pipe maker who I want to see and a museum or university that she wants to see.

Carole is part Danish, and for many years she wanted to visit her relatives in Copenhagen. Once I discovered the high-grade Danish pipes, I suddenly wanted to visit Copenhagen too. During the day, while she spends time with her Danish cousins, I get to see some of my favorite pipe makers. Then we might meet up for a dinner in which we are both excited about our adventures of the day and swap stories, laugh and otherwise have a fantastic time.

Our daughter Sara lives in suburban New York City, her husband works on Wall Street, and as of now they have two beautiful children: Scott, who was born in early 2010, and Lillian, born in late 2011. Being a grandpa is one of the highlights of my life. I cannot put into words how much joy, fun and sheer pleasure those little kids give me! This is why I used the photo that I did, with Sara's permission, at the start of this chapter.

Then there is the question of good health. Sigmund

Freud said work and love are the keys to happiness, and I believe he was correct, assuming we agree that good health is a prerequisite for both. Without good health, all the success, creativity, monetary achievement and love in the world are meaningless. Good health is the foundation for a happy life.

That is why I keep reminding myself of the importance of limiting my pipe smoking to two or three bowls a day, and no inhaling! I use an exclamation point because, honestly, it is very easy to succumb to inhaling smoke, and it is very important to be conscious of this fact and not do it. I also make a vigorous exercise program and sensible diet part of my goals for a balanced life. I am not saying you must follow my example; I'm just telling you what I do to try to stay youthful and energetic in my 60s.

There is a terrific book that I highly recommend called "Younger Next Year" by Chris Crowley and Henry S. Lodge, a heart patient who is a good writer and his cardiologist. They really sell the benefits of lifting weights as well as aerobics for living a long and happy life. They also stress the importance of social interaction and the feeling of community, which makes pipe collecting an ideal hobby because of our many pipe shows and pipe clubs.

I love listening to motivational speakers like Louise Hay, who is in her 80s and says this is the best decade of her life. She also suggests that all of us make whatever decade we are in "the best decade of your life." For me, my 60s, which is actually my seventh decade, is my best ever!

W. Clement Stone was an insurance magnate in Chicago who devoted much of his time to spreading the message of the importance of having PMA, which stands for a "Positive Mental Attitude." I particularly like Stone because he was never without his cigar and lived to be 100, which he had set as his goal.

As I have said repeatedly, pipe smoking helps me unwind and relax. It is better than any tranquilizer and more helpful than yoga for me. As long as I don't inhale and limit my consumption to moderate levels, I feel terrific -- full of life and energy -- with a calmness and serenity that is unique in today's world.

A number of writers in our hobby have jokingly referred to Pipe Acquisition Disorder (PAD), which is the condition of compulsive pipe buying that gets out of control, so that the collector risks the family's milk money with his excessive pipe purchases, loses his job, and possibly his marriage, and otherwise destroys his life. I don't know of anyone who has gone that far, though I suspect there are some.

Buying beautiful and hard-to-find pipes can be a little like compulsive gambling if you don't consciously discipline yourself to show restraint. Of course, common sense must prevail.

The same for arguments and debates among hobbyists, where all of us -- myself included -- appear to go ballistic over what in the end are the tiniest and most inconsequential points. Once we get on our keyboards or in front of an audience, however, many of us seem to be grandstanding for the audience. I have had any number of polite and interesting conversations with some of the people who have attacked my views, and, believe it or not, we get along famously.

Faith is an important part of my life, especially as I have gotten older and seen so many good friends die. The one that hit me hardest was my mother's death on September 2, 2011. Her name was Ann Lombard Newcombe, and she lived 88 years filled with love, faith and optimism. She was truly a saint -- incredibly warm, kind and supportive -- always encouraging all eight of her children to do what we loved to do. She was joined at the hip with my father for 65 years, had a wonderful sense of humor, and always figured out how to turn hard work into fun.

That is a marvelous trait to develop, and it is common among high achievers. I remember once meeting with the media mogul Rupert Murdoch in his New York apartment in 1984, and he was about to go on a skiing vacation in Aspen. He gave me his private phone number at his home there and told me to call him if I had any questions about what we were discussing, and I said, "Don't worry, I won't bother you on your vacation," and his then-wife Anna replied, "Are you kidding? You have to understand that Rupert's work is his play."

I have always remembered that and tried to make my work my play.

And it is how I view everything to do with pipes ... play. When I think of that word, I think of fun, relaxation, excitement and all those other feelings that come from feeling good.

That is why I smoke a pipe, and it is why I love pipe collecting so much -- to feel good! But if I find myself overdoing it, or allowing my interest in pipes to take over the other areas of my life, I always remind myself of my goals for a balanced life and pull back.

Of course, this can require discipline, just as the achievement of all important goals -- whether for career, family or fitness -- requires discipline and hard work. But it is worth the effort.

I am a great believer in positive self-talk at all times, and I find the more encouraged I feel, the more prone I am to encourage other people. This is one of the reasons I love looking at other people's pipe collections, to see what appeals to them when they can choose from a nearly infinite variety of options.

But with as many choices as there are, you have to remember that almost all pipe shapes are variations on a handful of classical shapes. They represent the pipe maker's interpretation of the classics. That is why I disagree when some of the old-time pipe makers criticize the newer ones for making pipes in similar shapes. As Picasso said, "Bad artists copy. Good artists steal." Bo Nordh used a Scandinavian expression, "I steal with my arms and legs," which translated means, "I steal with everything I've got."

My pipe collector friends span all ages -- from their 20s to their 80s -- and I just love that aspect of the hobby. Age means nothing when it comes to pipes. I have lengthy conversations with pipe enthusiasts who are younger than my children, and I feel like we are absolute equals because of our shared "passion for pipes." In fact, I never think about how old they are, because it is totally and completely irrelevant to the conversation.

You might be interested to know that I first heard the phrase "a passion for pipes" in 1996 when we were planning a family vacation to South Africa. This was before Google and the digital revolution had shrunk the world, though the groundwork had been laid through deregulation and it was not so unusual for an American family to visit Africa. My wife contacted the tobacconist Sturk's in Johannesburg, and she wanted to know if there were enthusiastic collectors in the city.

"Yes," he said, "we have a few who have a real passion for pipes, so I'm sure your husband will fit right in."

After she told me that, I wrote down the phrase and said, if I ever write a book about pipes, that alliterative phrase could make a catchy title. Then when I finally did write my first book, I settled on the concept of "pipe dreams," figuring I could always use the "passion for pipes" phrase in a future book. But as I waited, I watched Neill Archer Roan set up his website under that moniker. I love the phrase and was happy that someone was smart enough to use it.

The meditation and thoughtful analysis that a relaxed pipe bowl can bring is like nothing else, provided that it is done in moderation and as part of a balanced lifestyle. The same is true when it comes to the excitement and exhilaration of making new acquisitions for your collection.

It is not always easy to lead a balanced life, and your goals and interests should flow from within you, from what gets you passionate -- from your own personal "pipe dreams." My only advice is to stress how important it is to keep your pipe smoking and collecting in perspective, to use them to round out an otherwise fulfilling lifestyle.

CHAPTER TWELVE

~~~~~

PIPES AND CHINA IN 2011

A men's restroom sign at the Port of Shanghai could be understood in any country or language. The women's restroom sign was a stiletto high heel.

The growing Chinese market is affecting the economy of every nation around the world. I can't think of any commercial activity that has escaped the influence of this vast market, and that includes the market for pipes.

Since I had an opportunity to visit China in August of 2011, I paid particular attention to what was happening in the world of pipes. I had been to Beijing in 2000, and there was virtually no market for high grade pipes. But in 11 years, like so many other industries and businesses, there was sudden interest in China.

* * * * *

If you want to understand what is happening in the world of pipes today, you need to go to China.

The Chinese have affected every aspect of pipe collecting worldwide, especially by driving up prices, but they are also providing a much-needed safety net for many pipe makers and transforming the hobby by bringing a new level of energy and enthusiasm into what had become a fairly predictable marketplace. Whether this is a permanent or temporary change remains to be seen.

I visited Shanghai in August 2011 and was greeted by Leslie Ng, who has been called the "Pipe Pope of China" because he founded and runs Pipevillage.org, which has been described as the most important portal for Chinese smokers, collectors and distributors all over the world. Leslie has strong opinions. He loves a good debate on the Internet, and he is not afraid to speak his mind.

He also owns the label "Gloredo," which makes pipes and pipe accessories. I feel a special fondness for the brilliant 32-year-old because he translated my first book, "In Search of Pipe Dreams," into Chinese and published it as a coffee-table book with magnificent color photos. In fact, in my extremely biased opinion, it is the most beautiful pipe book ever published because of the high quality photographs and printing. (At the same time, it is a strange feeling to write an entire book and not be able to read a word of it.)

Leslie had arranged for a book-signing event at Wilson's pipe store, which is named C-Pipes. Several days before the event, Leslie, Wilson and I had a wonderful lunch of Shanghainese-Cantonese fusion food, which I happen to love. We were served one dish after another, which we shared, and it was delicious.

Wilson was surprised that I was so fond of Chinese food, especially since many of the European pipe makers are not. He said the Italians in particular complain about the food in China.

But it's not just the cooking that I like about modern China. The trains run on time, the platforms and cars are immaculate, and the streets are clean and safe. The people are friendly and industrious. Shanghai is like a combination of New York and Las Vegas, only cleaner than both.

My wife, Carole, and I had dinner at a restaurant where the Chinese waiter had just returned home to Shanghai after having worked in Boston for 13 years. "I love Boston," he said, "and there was some growth in the city during that time. But you see those skyscrapers?" he asked, pointing to a section called Pudong New District that features one skyscraper after another, reminding me of the Chicago skyline. "When I left for the States in 1998, that area was mostly a rural village. All the growth has occurred since that time."

Something similar has happened with pipes. All of the growth has occurred during the past decade, and particularly during the past five years. Chinese pipe smokers regularly buy from American and European pipe sellers. They also buy from the many Chinese pipe sellers who have opened their doors for business since 2005.

Wilson's is a good example. He opened his store in 2007 and sells 30 pipes a day, seven days a week, through the store or on-line. He is also a wholesaler who provides pipes to stores throughout China, so this means selling thousands more pipes every year. Can you imagine the enormous demand he has for quality inventory? It is staggering.

And he is only one of the many incredible pipe sellers in China. Mr. Lin in Shenzhen has come to the Chicago show to buy pipes, as has Eddie Wong. Some of the other sellers in China include Mr. Song in Fuzhou and Mr. Feng in Beijing. This helps explain why prices have gone up. They need more high grade pipes than the pipe makers can make.

When I visited the Tinder Box in Santa Monica after this summer's IPCPR national tobacco convention, Leo Reyes, the manager, told me that there were many beautiful pipes but he couldn't understand why the prices seemed so much higher than in past years. The only reason would be if there were more buyers for those pipes. Of course, maybe there has been an increase in America, Europe, Japan and other areas, but without a doubt China has been a major contributor to this growth.

Wilson said the moderately-priced Italian pipes are his best sellers, while his most expensive pipes are the high-grade Danish. I asked about American pipe makers, and he said a few of them are starting to become noticed in China, but it's still early. I predicted that their recognition is just a matter of time.

When we were eating lunch, Wilson casually mentioned that he is selling an unsmoked Bo Nordh calabash with an ivory cap. I asked the price, and he said $30,000, which he pointed out is inexpensive compared with the cost of great works of art. I told Wilson and Leslie the story of how, in 1993, I had turned down an identical pipe offered for $2,400 because I thought it was too expensive!

Personally, I have given up on acquiring a Bo Nordh calabash, unless the prices some day fall to where they were in the 1980s. Fat chance -- but you never know. Imagine, however, if you were Bo Nordh and you were paid maybe $1,200 for a pipe that was later sold for $30,000. Now you can understand why artisan pipe makers sometimes find it difficult to hit the right prices. We collectors tell them their prices are too high, but then when something like this occurs, where the distributors and sellers are making $28,800 and you -- the pipe maker -- are only getting $1,200 for the pipe you made, it does not seem fair.

I should point out that Wilson is only asking market prices. He is extremely fair in his dealings, and we have seen sellers in Europe get similar prices for certain Bo Nordh pipes, and it is likely that other Chinese sellers have as well. My point is that this explosive growth in prices in a worldwide market, driven by globalization, the Internet and the vast number of Chinese pipe buyers, is a relatively new phenomenon.

In the meanwhile, in my own quest for a high-grade calabash, I have turned to Tonni Nielsen, the Danish pipe maker who lives in Kentucky but also has a home in Denmark. Tonni is my favorite calabash pipe maker these days. He makes a variety of calabashes, and the lines on his pipes, as well as the detail, demonstrate what a master artisan he is. His calabash pipes are made both with a removable cap and as one piece. I bought one of these pipes at last year's West Coast Pipe Show for $1,000, which is expensive, yes, but an absolute steal compared with trying to buy one of Bo Nordh's calabashes. The pipe that I have is a one-piece calabash with the crown being unstained briar. The execution of the shape and stain are flawless, and I know that Bo would have been mightily impressed. Elegant is the word that best describes Tonni Nielsen's calabashes.

I told all this to Wilson at lunch, and I had the feeling that he would contact Tonni that night and order as many calabashes as he could make. Let's say that I'm right and that happened. Imagine being Tonni Nielsen and getting that order. Can you see why this new Chinese business is great for the pipe makers?

There was a time, not so long ago, when Tonni gave tennis lessons to supplement his income, and Tom Eltang was making furniture as well as pipes. But despite tough times, they persisted in making pipes out of a love for the craft. Jess Chonowitsch once told me that he remembers telling Lars Ivarsson, during a rough stretch, that they could turn the lights out but they would still be pipe makers no matter what. I remember attending an RTDA convention in

Chicago in the mid-90's and watching Teddy Knudsen trying very hard to persuade pipe store owners to buy his pipes. Now, Teddy has orders totaling many thousands of dollars and the demand is much greater than he can supply.

Not all of this is due to China, of course. The boom in demand for high grade pipes began more than a decade ago, but it's just that a market as vast as China, with very intelligent and aggressive Chinese pipe sellers, has put the sales of high grade pipes on steroids.

Some pipe smokers would argue that this is a negative development because it is raising the prices of their pipes. But I think the benefits -- enthusiasm for the hobby and security for the pipe makers -- have led to even more beautiful pipes, and, ultimately, to more choices of great pipes for the collector. It is also possible that this is only a temporary development and prices will come down in the future. We simply don't know.

Wilson had promoted the book-signing event on his website, complete with my picture and promotional copy that of course I was unable to read. At the last minute, however, he encountered an emergency and was unable to host or even attend the event. But he and Leslie made arrangements with another pipe store owner, Mr. Ju (pronounced "Mr. Gee"), and the customers were directed from one store to the other. Besides being a very nice man, Mr. Ju is another successful pipe seller who, according to Leslie, is averaging 600-plus pipe sales per month, mainly on the Internet.

I met more than a dozen Chinese collectors who could not have been friendlier or more interesting. They reminded me of the pipe smokers I see at American and European pipe shows -- we all have the same questions, concerns and interests.

One very impressive collector whose English was impeccable was Wilfred Feng, a scientist and consultant in Shanghei who works for a Washington, D.C.-based law firm. He is very familiar with America since he travels here at least twice a year. Wilfred told me that he switched to a pipe as a way to give up cigarettes, and I said that was exactly why I started smoking a pipe.

"It is difficult to smoke in your country," he said, and I couldn't disagree.

This brings up the question of freedom -- all types of freedom. I am concerned that my libertarian friends might think that, with all this praise of China, I've gone soft on communism. I have not. I hate communism and everything about it. But what I saw in Shanghai was capitalism, not communism. You don't build a Manhattan-like skyline in a dozen years by government decree. If that were the case, we'd see them in Cuba and North Korea. In fact, when China was governed by pure communism, Shanghai was largely a wasteland compared with what it is today.

It is important to note, however, that the Chinese approach to civil liberties is still very different from that in America or Europe. Their concept of freedom is not ours. Beyond that, I won't pretend to be an expert or to offer a blanket endorsement of their system, by any means.

But what about the resentment we see from some Americans who think "made in China" is synonymous with cheap labor and shoddy workmanship? With such explosive growth, it is inevitable that corners will be cut at times, and no doubt we can all find examples to bolster those sentiments. But we can also find examples of cut corners on products that are "made in America." That is the danger of trying to judge individuals or products by nationality rather than individually.

As for pipe products made in China, the only ones I am familiar with are the ones Leslie supervises, and I guarantee you that the Gloredo pipe cleaners are fantastic. They are offered for sale by smokingpipes.com, and they are my personal favorites. Gloredo also offers beautiful looking pipes and very nice leather pipe bags, both of which will be coming to America soon.

Wilson said he heard rumblings that officials of the Chicago Pipe Show were unhappy that the Chinese buyers out-bid many collectors and walked away with the entire inventory of various pipe makers. He asked what I thought about that, and I said I could see both sides. If an American collector from Iowa, for example, traveled to the Chicago show to buy an Ilsted pipe and was told that the Chinese had bought all of Poul's pipes before the official show even began, then I can understand that collector's frustration and anger.

But if I were Poul Ilsted and I could sell everything I made in one fell swoop, and avoid haggling, indecision, possible criticism and all the other hassles that accompany selling one pipe at a time, it makes perfect sense. Besides, that collector from Iowa could always special-order an Ilsted pipe directly from Poul, and he would gladly make it.

It is not only the Chinese, however, who are affecting prices. Kurt Balleby sold his entire inventory at a recent Chicago show to Russian buyers. What we are really talking about is globalization. But since there are so many Chinese, they obviously have the upper hand in any type of mini-trade war among pipe buyers and sellers.

What does the future hold? Will this Chinese influence grow and continue to drive up prices and make certain high grade pipes less available to the rest of us? After all, it is a country of more than 1.3 billion people (as compared with .3 for America), and this newfound enthusiasm for high-grade pipes could be just the beginning.

The argument against that lies with an understanding of the business cycle that is a reality of life in all capitalist societies. There are periods of credit expansion and contraction -- boom and bust -- and we are obviously talking about a prolonged boom that is bound to cool off in time.

While writing this article, I corresponded with an American pipe collector who travels regularly to China, and he predicted that the current state of affairs will not last. Writing about the Chinese, he said, "It seems they have a huge appetite for all things from the West right now. I think the inevitable collapse is coming." He also said that in his experience, "the Chinese rabidly pursue something, quickly lose interest and move onto something else."

I thought back to a pipe show I attended in Germany several years ago when I met an enthusiastic Chinese pipe seller named Echo, who showed me his very beautiful book about pipes. I was so impressed. But when I asked Leslie about Echo, he said he is mainly selling single malt whiskey these days.

So which will it be? A permanent increase in pipe prices or a temporary intrusion into the world of pipes that we knew in the past? Your guess is as good as mine. But with the whole world looking down their noses at smokers, the fact that a growing number of Chinese are joining the brotherhood of the briar should be seen as good news, and I believe they should be embraced with open arms by all of us who truly love our pipes and, in a manner of speaking, our pipe comrades.

CHAPTER THIRTEEN

~~~~~

IS IT ALL IN MY HEAD?

A young Sixten Ivarsson was much in demand for his classically-shaped pipes long before he started a revolution with freehand shapes.

This chapter was written after my visit to Denmark in October 2011, and it addresses the question of whether certain brands of pipes smoke better than others. Of course, we will never come up with a definitive answer, and there is nothing wrong with that, because it's always fun to speculate.

I quote Former's telling the story of how he discovered the contrast staining technique for pipes, though I must point out that other pipe makers have claimed credit for being the ones to have made this discovery as well. I don't know that it really matters if several people discovered the same technique at around the same time, but I found Former's story to be plausible and interesting.

* * * * *

Two men were standing at a bus stop in Copenhagen on a crisp autumn morning in 1950. One pulled out his pipe and, as he was filling it with tobacco, the other said, "I am so envious. I dropped my favorite pipe last night, and it broke."

"That's no problem," said the other, as he was lighting his pipe. "There is a young man who has a special gift for making pipes and repairing broken ones. His name is Sixten Ivarsson. If you bring him your pipe, I'm sure he can fix it for you or make you a new one that will smoke even better."

That conversation, or similar ones, took place thousands of times between the years 1947 and 1959, the years before Sixten Ivarsson created his first freehand pipe. Sixten is known today as the inventive genius who paved the way for hundreds of pipe artisans by creating "functional art." Much has been written about the artistic side, and no doubt that has inspired a small army of young pipe makers.

But it is the functional side that interests me most. This is because I became so passionate about Sixten's pipes, not because of their beauty or daring designs, but because they smoked so well. I bought my first one out of curiosity. I had heard he made great pipes, and I found one that was very beautiful. That was in 1989, about a dozen years after I had been a pipe smoker. The pipe was a revelation when I started smoking it. I could not remember any pipe smoking so well.

This led me to buy more Ivarsson pipes, and, six years later, to travel to Denmark to meet the great master himself, to befriend his son Lars, and granddaughter Nanna (Lars' daughter), as well as Bo Nordh and Jess Chonowitsch. Jess, incidentally -- and impressively -- was the only non-family member permitted to make some pipes stamped "An Ivarsson Product."

I wrote enthusiastically about these pipes and stressed their unique smoking qualities, despite a sizable opinion in the pipe community that the "unique smoking qualities" belief was all in my head. In fact, there would appear to be a consensus among experienced pipe collectors and pipe makers, and even some pipe sellers, that well made pipes all smoke essentially the same. The reason some pipes cost more than others is because they are perceived to be beautiful, or rare, or some factor other than their smoking qualities.

Fortunately, I have steadfastly stayed in the minority (if it is a minority) in disagreeing with this belief. I say "fortunately" because I started collecting pipes made by Ivarsson, Nordh and Chonowitsch primarily because of their smoking qualities, with the beauty of their designs being of secondary consideration, long before the prices for these pipes soared into the stratosphere.

But how is it possible, you might ask, that certain brands of pipes smoke better than others? After all, if pipes are drilled according to the same dimensions, then they should smoke the same. Peter Heding, who earned his PhD in biology and was a medical researcher before becoming a pipe maker, said that as a scientist, it makes sense to him that pipes drilled to the exact same specifications, with identically comfortable mouthpieces, would smoke the same, whether they are made by an artisan or at a factory.

Many other pipe makers, including the truly talented

Tom Eltang, have said that a well-made factory pipe smokes just as well as a super high-grade. Many pipe smokers have reached similar conclusions. As my much-missed friend and mentor Ed Lehman used to say, "When it comes to collecting pipes, Rick, a good smoker is a given. They are all good smokers. But we chase after certain ones because they are unique or hard to find or beautiful, or maybe they fit in with the motif of our collection."

Even some pipe sellers have made similar comments. For instance, Rob Cooper says that he collects old Larsen pipes to display for their beauty, but if he wants a great smoke, he'll fire up an old, well-made factory pipe, usually a bulldog.

Collecting pipes for their beauty is commonplace now, and it seems that much of the collecting world has moved in the direction of pipe sculpture. Tom Looker is probably the most outspoken champion of this development, and Tom's displays of pipes as great works of art are breathtaking. I had no idea that pipes could be turned into sculptural artwork that would enhance any mantelpiece.

The two pipe makers whose work Tom displays most often are Tokutomi and Teddy Knudsen, both of whom served lengthy apprenticeships making classical pipes. They both are indisputably master pipe makers, unlike, I suspect, the majority of newer pipe makers who make sculptural pipes rather than classics.

Tom recently asked me why I had not gotten more involved with these pipes, and I didn't have a good answer except that, as we were having this conversation, I was really enjoying puffing on the chubby apple-shaped pipe that Jess Chonowitsch had made. To me, Jess' pipe was beautiful and a fantastic smoker. It is comfortable in my hand and mouth, while I cannot imagine smoking a pipe that would belong on my mantelpiece.

Steven Van Puyvelde is a young pipe collector from Belgium who has become an enthusiastic collector of Nanna pipes. What he finds so interesting about her pipes, and those of Lars, Jess and Bang, is that "they are art objects which are functional too, which requires a special skill to make complex art look simple so that the pipe is a great smoker." As Leonardo da Vinci said, "Simplicity is the ultimate sophistication."

Since beauty is in the eye of the beholder, it is wonderful that Tom Looker and I can be friends while being equally passionate about two totally different standards of perfection in pipe making. I am drawn to beautiful pipes as much as Tom is, but my ideal of beauty can be seen in classically-shaped bowls that are enhanced by the pipe maker's unique interpretation, with special emphasis being placed on the pipe being a good smoker.

Lars Ivarsson epitomizes my ideal in this regard. He made or worked on hundreds of billiard bowls in his early years and gradually created the brandy glass bowl as his unique interpretation, which is my personal favorite. Rounded-bowl bent pipes at some point became a blowfish, one of his most brilliant creations. I find it fascinating that these two shapes, the brandy bowl and blowfish, have become classics in their own right. This is not only because they are so beautiful, but also because they lend themselves to being great smokers.

I visited Lars in October 2011 only a few days before his trip to China in which he was to be honored, along with Nanna, for their family tradition of three generations of pipe making. They had uncovered some old photos of a young Sixten in his workshop that would be displayed in China as well.

Lars is meticulous in his pipe making, and he had spent the previous 10 weeks making the 10 pipes he was bringing. They were simply stunning -- my idea of what a masterpiece looks like -- and each one could be described as a freehand that was rooted in a classical shape; meaning, each one was designed to be a great smoker, yet they were incredibly inviting as works of art.

I asked Lars about the many newer pipe makers from all over the world, whether he thought they were putting art ahead of function. He said yes.

"Don't forget, my father spent more than a decade doing repairs and making classical pipes," he said. "He developed a large following during that time. People liked the way his pipes smoked."

It was not until 1959 that Sixten decided to make a horn-shaped pipe because it seemed like such a natural outgrowth from the lines on a block of briar. The problem was that the shape would not fit into the lathe.

"So he drilled the holes by hand," Lars said, "and he realized that he could do this with many different shapes. That was the beginning of his freehand creations."

Lars and I were having this conversation over a dinner that he and his wife, Annette, prepared mainly with ingredients that they grew themselves. Everything was so delicious that Lars could have become a master chef if he had wanted. Also at dinner were my wife, Carole, and Nanna and her absolutely adorable 3-year-old son, Sixten.

Lars was amused by the fact that most people in the hobby today don't seem to realize that his father's creative shapes came so many years after he had established his reputation as a master craftsman of classically-shaped pipes that were incredible smokers. Lars started the same way -- doing repairs and making classical pipes. Nanna did the same.

Lars is a great admirer of Japanese culture and art, and he pointed out that a sculptor-in-training might be given a thousand pounds of clay and told to make 60 identical sake cups. If there were the slightest flaw or variation in one, it would be thrown out. That helps explain why pipes made by Sixten, Lars and Nanna smoke so well. Every small detail is meticulously addressed.

As the architect Mies van der Rohe famously said, "God is in the details."

What about Fred Hanna's theory, subscribed to by many in the pipe community, including high-profile collectors Greg Pease and Regis McCafferty, that the briar is a more important factor than brand in determining whether a pipe is a good smoker?

I once asked Bo Nordh what he thought of that, and he replied that he had 30 pipes in his personal collection -- the ones he smoked -- and of those, the three best smokers were definitely better than the rest, and another three were decidedly inferior to the rest, "while the remaining 24 are just plain old Bo Nordh pipes." In other words, in Bo's opinion, they were fantastic smokers, but the difference in briar had a definite influence on the top and bottom 10 percent. That makes sense to me.

Antonio Stradivari was known as one of the most skilled artisans of all time -- a true genius in his workshop. The London newspaper, The Independent, once described him as "perhaps the most revered craftsman in world history." Stradivarius violins are considered by many experts to be superior to all others, yet scholars have debated for centuries what qualities in their construction made them so special.

It is safe to say that most experts agree that it was some combination of skill, artistry, attention to detail and the wood itself, including how it was treated. No one can say for sure what the defining factors were, but it makes sense that everything came together in the Stradivarius workshop.

In the same way, I don't think we can state definitively what are the most important factors in explaining why certain pipes are great smokers. Yet I can't help but be struck by the fact that Sixten Ivarsson received such an enthusiastic reception -- from thousands of individual pipe smokers, solely by word-of-mouth with no media attention whatsoever -- for his classically-shaped pipes made with the same briar that all the other pipe makers were using.

Remember, these were classical pipes with ordinary briar, and everyone was raving about them. If "brand" is not the most important factor -- meaning, who made the pipe -- why was there a waiting list to buy them?

There are so many newer pipe makers today, and the majority are enthralled with the fancy shapes. With some, their attitude is, the crazier the better. I like elegant shapes (though not too fancy), but my overriding concern is with finding pipes that are great smokers.

It was for this reason that I wanted to see Hans "Former" Nielsen on this trip. I had acquired five Former pipes over the years, and every time I smoked one, I thought, "What a great pipe!" When I told this to Former in his spacious workshop, which is located 75 kilometers outside Copenhagen, his face lit up. He said that the worst thing he can hear is if someone buys one of his pipes to display in a glass case.

Former started his career by working for the brilliant pipe maker Poul Rasmussen at Suhr's pipe store in Copenhagen. For two years he did nothing but repair mouthpieces on customers' pipes, or make them new ones. This was excellent training before he was hired to make pipes for W.O. Larsen. He joined Larsen when Svend Bang was in charge of the workshop. Bang left shortly thereafter to set up his own pipe and tobacco store, and he eventually hired Per Hansen and Ulf Noltensmeier to make what became the world-famous Bang pipes.

Former remembers Sixten Ivarsson knocking on the window of the workshop, which was next door to the Larsen store, and waving hello in the morning on his way to work at his own workshop 300 yards down the street. He remembers a young and very serious Bo Nordh intently watching him work, taking mental notes, and asking one question after another. He remembers his close friend Sven Knudsen, Teddy's older brother, and their many pipe making adventures. He remembers working with, and helping, many younger pipe makers who went on to achieve world-class status in their own right, including Jess Chonowitsch, Poul Ilsted and Tonni Nielsen.

"Too many of the newer pipe makers have never learned how to make classical pipes," he said. "There are times when I look at eBay and the high prices for pipes that will not smoke well, and I think, 'that is money-making, not pipe-making.'"

Former will turn 70 on his next birthday, but his

passion for pipe making keeps him youthful. You'd think he was 20 years younger. He has never been a self-promoter, and he has remained loyal to his pipe sellers who believed in him from the beginning.

Carole and I had lunch with Former and his charming wife, Daniella, who is from Switzerland and speaks four languages, including -- according to Former -- better Danish than he does, and he is the one who grew up in Denmark! Daniella also does the final polishing on all Former pipes.

While at lunch I learned one fact that was absolutely astounding: It was Former who created the double-contrast stain, which has revolutionized the display and appeal of pipes for nearly half a century.

The year was 1962, and Former was frustrated that the water-based stains that all pipe makers were using failed to enhance the grain in a dramatic fashion. One day he passed a store window and saw a poster advertising alcohol-based leather dyes that were guaranteed to soak into the leather of shoes and leave a lasting stain.

He bought a small bottle of black dye as an experiment, took it home and stained a raw-wood pipe solid black. The next day he sanded off the stain and -- Eureka! -- the result was just what he was hoping for. The black had soaked into the soft parts of the wood, which meant that the lines of the straight grain, and the dots of the bird's eye, stood out in sharp contrast. He then stained the entire bowl a light orange, making it a "double contrast," and the modern-looking pipe of today was born.

This was a discovery that has been copied millions of times by nearly every pipe maker and pipe factory all over the world, and it was Former who was responsible. Talk about a monumental achievement! What is even more impressive is that Former has never once sought recognition for his discovery. He casually mentioned it over lunch while saying that he would blush at the prices that self-promoting pipe makers are charging for their pipes these days.

Now I am not advocating a false sense of humility, nor did I detect any of that in Former. He has a healthy self-esteem and knows that his pipes are good. In fact, when I asked him if he thought his pipes smoked better than most others, he smiled and said, "of course," which is what every pipe maker should believe about his own pipes.

I also should point out that, in addition to Former's dramatic discovery, other pipe makers experimented with their own forms of contrast staining. Lars Ivarsson said that Sixten was impressed by the staining used at one of the British pipe-making factories in the late 1950s. After some experimentation, he found something called a "laboratory stain" that is copper-based and combines two components. It is highly toxic when used, but totally harmless after being applied to the wood. Lars has used this stain his entire career.

During this same trip to Denmark, I spent time at the Bang workshop in Copenhagen, which is always a treat. Just sitting there with Ulf and Per, slowly puffing on our pipes -- all Bangs, of course -- is a Zen-like experience. Ulf and Per both said that making great smoking pipes has always been just as important to them as making pipes that are beautiful.

Ulf said that 10 years ago the first question in every interview was, "'When you retire, who will continue the tradition of pipe making?' No one asks us that anymore because there are so many new pipe makers, and they are all over the world."

Per said he did not like the fact that everyone was copying everyone. "If you do nothing but copy other people's work, it is soulless. It's just a copy, and it's just for money. A great pipe maker must have passion for his own ideas."

Per is correct, no doubt, in a perfect world, but the problem today is money. Wealthy buyers from China, Russia, the United States, Germany and other countries have driven up the prices so that the average collector who wants a high grade can find it very difficult to acquire one. You should not have to spend thousands of dollars to get a great smoking pipe. That would be ridiculous.

But I have seen the prices for some of the high grades

that I am writing about climb from $350 to $1,500 to $3,500 and more -- and sometimes a lot more.

Personally, I have extremely conflicted feelings about this. As a friend of the pipe makers, and as a collector with a sizable number of these pipes (one-third of which were acquired for $350 or less), I am all for the soaring prices.

But I'm really not. As a friend of many pipe collectors, and as one who always wants to buy new pipes, I wish the prices would drop dramatically -- so everyone reading this could try these pipes.

One solution would be for the newer pipe makers, presumably at much lower prices, to offer pipes that have an emphasis on good smoking qualities, as opposed to being "works of art." Not everyone can make high grade pipes that are good smokers, but I wish they'd try. If they want to copy the masters, they should copy the inside of their pipes -- how they are engineered and all the tiny details of craftsmanship that someone like Lars puts into each pipe -- rather than the designs.

The problem is that in the short run the fancy pipes are considered "high grades" and are the ones that command the highest prices. But if they are not great smokers, the high prices will not last. I remember 20 years ago at pipe shows there were sculptural pipes by Micoli that sold for $1,500. Today, those same pipes sell for something like $50 on eBay.

What sways the pipe smoker market over the long run is quality -- not just beauty or art, but function; meaning, how well a pipe maker's pipes smoke, how comfortable they are in the hand and mouth, and -- most importantly -- how often the pipe smoker keeps reaching for pipes made by that pipe maker.

A master pipe maker recognizes that making great smoking pipes is his most important challenge. As Former said, "What I care about most is that my customers enjoy smoking my pipes. That is the test to determine if I have succeeded as a pipe maker."

If all well-made pipes smoke the same, then why is

Former's goal to make pipes that his customers enjoy smoking?

I think the answer is obvious: He does not believe that all well-made pipes smoke the same. He believes that some pipes smoke better than others, and he is totally committed to making the best smoking pipes possible.

Is it all in my head that some brands of pipes smoke better than most other pipes?

Is it all in the heads of great pipe makers that they want to make the best smoking pipes possible, better than other well-made pipes?

Of course I don't think so. But even if it is, it makes no difference in the end, because whenever I smoke one of these pipes, I feel transported to a different place, one characterized by contentment, serenity and total relaxation, which is what pipe smoking is all about.

Whenever I hear that all well-made pipes smoke the same -- and I know for myself that has not been my experience -- I am tempted to say, "OK, whatever you say," and then to settle back and enjoy my pipes, knowing that I am in another world.

CHAPTER FOURTEEN

TELL ME WHAT YOU LIKE

I don't consider myself an expert at pipes, except for knowing what I like, but I am without a doubt an expert at optimism and enthusiasm.

This final chapter summarizes my philosophy of pipe collecting, which is to focus enthusiastically on what you like. Obviously that is an important theme of this book. I presented this talk at the banquet dinner of the first West Coast Pipe Show in Las Vegas in November 2009. Pipe collecting is such a fun hobby when you focus on what appeals to you most. There is simply nothing like it in the world today.

* * * * *

One night after dinner with two pipe friends, we retired to my den to enjoy our pipes. My guests were the musical composer Lalo Schifrin and Los Angeles physician David Boska. After a few minutes of relaxed pipe smoking, I was so mellow that Dr. Boska asked, half joking, "Rick, do you want to go to sleep?"

"No," I replied. "I am just completely at peace. I am enjoying my pipe and our conversation. In fact, my mind is wide awake while my body is totally relaxed."

I have no doubt that if the good doctor had taken my blood pressure at that moment, it would have been in the ideal range.

"That's the amazing thing about pipe smoking," Dr. Boska said, while holding up his pipe. "It helps your body relax while simultaneously improving your mental clarity. What else does this?"

I wish more doctors thought that way. One reader of my first book sent me a fan letter from England saying that his father's doctor prescribed moderate pipe smoking rather than tranquilizers to help reduce stress in some of his patients. Considering the potential danger of tranquilizers, and the way they are dispensed so freely, that certainly makes sense to me.

On the subject of using the pipe for relaxation, I remember an incident that occurred last spring at a pipe show in Sparks, Nevada. It was during that quiet time between the closing of the doors on Saturday afternoon and dinner. While most people were in their rooms getting ready to go out, I found a comfortable table outside the bar where smoking was permitted. I settled down in a well-padded chair and lit my pipe.

Father Al Grosskopf, a Jesuit priest and passionate pipe collector for many years, joined me. I was smoking a new J. Alan pipe I had picked up earlier that day, while Father Al pulled out a beautiful S. Bang pipe he had bought recently in Switzerland. We both oohed and aahed over each other's pipes as we shared some old English pipe tobacco, comfortably ensconced in our chairs, enjoying the scenery and relaxing in a way that only pipe aficionados can truly appreciate.

Picture complete peace and quiet despite the hubbub and crowded slot machines around us. Total relaxation. A serene world far away from today's frantic comings and goings, where we were both content to take occasional puffs from our beloved pipes. We talked a little, but we also had moments of silence that are typical of pipe smokers who are lost in their pipe dreams.

This is nothing new. Peter Pan author J.M. Barrie, in his book "My Lady Nicotine," describes a scene in a London boarding house a hundred years ago in which he and his friends would gather in his room in the evening to enjoy their pipes. He said they would savor the Arcadia mixture in their pipes for long stretches of time without talking at all: "There was a ventilator in my room, which sometimes said 'Crik - crik!' reminding us that no one had spoken for half an hour."

As Father Al and I were lost in our reverie, a middle-aged man wearing a T-shirt and shorts came running over to us and stopped abruptly. He waved both hands in dramatic fashion to bring our pipe smoke toward his face, and he inhaled through his nose as deeply as possible.

With a contented, toothless grin, he said, "Now there's a sight you don't see every day, a couple of old coots smoking their pipes. I used to love smoking my pipe and really miss it."

"Who you callin' an 'old coot'?" Fr. Al replied, doing his best impression of Fred Sanford, the 1970s television character played by Redd Foxx.

It was obvious the man was joking, or at least partly joking, and we all had a good laugh.

But I tell this story because it relates to age. We associate pipe smoking with the elderly. It was not surprising that a college student recently quoted in The Wall Street Journal -- interviewed because it was so unusual that he smoked a pipe in the first place -- said that his friends were seeking their "inner child" while he was seeking his "inner old man."

Gary Schrier even wrote a book saying that he is part of the last generation of pipe smokers. Gary was 47 when he penned those words, in which he stated categorically: "pipes are dead."

I have two answers to this: the first is to say that you're as old as you feel, and the second is to observe the increasing number of young people who are getting involved in pipe shows, pipe making and pipe collecting -- people who were born after the last episode of Sanford and Son had been filmed in 1977.

Pipe smoking today requires a rebellious spirit. Rather than an "inner old man," I suspect most young pipe smokers are finding their "inner Huck Finn."

As for the first point, being as old as you feel, I believe moderate pipe smoking has calming effects that are irreplaceable. You simply won't find those benefits from any other source. That's why Ed Kolpin, founder of the original Tinder Box, became famous for saying, "You live longer with a pipe." Ed was an evangelist for pipe smoking until his death in 2007 at the youthful age of 97 -- and he was youthful his entire life.

Ed also took a lot of vitamins, as I have for many years. When I was in my 20s and living in Baltimore, I bought vitamins from a salesman in California named Freddie. Our conversations always began the same way:

"Freddie, how ya' doin'?"

"I feel great! If I felt any better, they'd have to put me in a cage!!!"

I loved that reply, especially considering that Freddie was 88 at the time.

There's no question that our attitude has a great deal to do with the aging process. We all know people who are 40 and act like they're 90, and we know older people who continue to be excited and enthusiastic about life. I love to see older pipe smokers who only late in life discover pipe shows, where they glow with the enthusiasm of youth.

I believe the key to staying young is to have an open-minded and optimistic attitude. If you feel genuinely enthusiastic about something, don't be afraid to act enthusiastic.

The pipe world is no different from anywhere else in that there are optimists and pessimists, and while both groups make convincing arguments, in the end, the optimists will prevail. They always do.

That's partly because pessimists give up while optimists persist. It is also because pessimists typically ignore the fact that when a door closes, a window opens.

There was a well-known European pipe writer who told me years ago that pipes were finished as a business, citing as proof the demise of two old English brands. He failed to notice the birth of many new brands, and new artisan pipe makers, from North America, Japan, China, Russia and the countries formerly known as Eastern Europe.

Then there was a high-grade pipe maker who, late at night in his living room, looking around as if his walls had ears, leaned over to whisper, "You're the only one I'll tell this to -- and please, don't let it get out -- but the high prices in today's market are unsustainable. We have never had them before, and we will never see them again." Since that hot tip, prices have continued to go up.

What about pipe publications? After Pipe Friendly closed, and after Tom Dunn died, and with him the Pipe Smoker's Ephemeris, we were left with two primary publications, Pipes and Tobaccos magazine and The Pipe

Collector newsletter. I have heard pessimistic collectors bemoan the loss of the first two publications and then bad-mouth the latter two, predicting they won't last long. I first heard these predictions more than a dozen years ago, and it is remarkable -- a cause for celebration -- that both publications continue to come out regularly with interesting reading for pipe enthusiasts.

Also, since those predictions were first made, we have seen the publication of many pipe books. The fact that all forms of print media are in decline gets past the pessimistic pipe collector. He is convinced it is pipes, not publishing, that are the problem. But if that were the case, then there would be no interest in pipes on the Internet.

In reality, there has been an explosion of pipe websites, blogs and forums on the Internet during the past few years. Remember, only a decade ago there were hardly any. Today, there are so many that it would be a full-time job just to keep up with all of them. And don't forget pipesmagazine.com. Kevin Godbee is doing a fantastic job with this online magazine, which was his brain child.

OK, but what about the very real problem of so many brick-and-mortar shops closing? Does this mean a corresponding decline in pipe sales? Not necessarily. It means that thousands of pipes are sold all over the world on eBay and through other electronic methods. As Tony Soderman says, "With eBay, we can attend a pipe show every day."

Now I am raising the issue of optimism versus pessimism for personal reasons. This is because I do not consider myself an expert at pipes -- except when it comes to my own pipe collection. I do consider myself an expert at optimism because I know what I like, and I can't resist sharing my enthusiasm, and for me, this hobby just keeps getting better and better.

When I read a great book, I am one of those people who tells everyone else, "You're gonna love this book!" When I see a movie that I like, I encourage everyone I meet to go see it. That's just my nature.

Well, this is precisely what happened with my pipe collecting. For many years I enjoyed pipes made mostly in England, Italy and America. Then I discovered Sixten Ivarsson pipes, and I liked them so much that I needed to find out more about them. I searched for pipes that smoked as well, for me, as his pipes did. I traveled to Scandinavia and met with Sixten, Lars and Nanna Ivarsson, Jess Chonowitsch, Bo Nordh and the S. Bang pipe makers, Per Hansen and Ulf Noltensmeier. I just loved the "Great Dane" pipes -- how they looked and how they smoked.

So what did I do? I told the world! I was not content simply to enjoy them. I wanted to share my experiences with anyone who would listen.

And frankly I wish more pipe collectors would do the same when it comes to their favorite pipes. There are a few examples now, and I think they're wonderful. For instance, I love it when Tony Pascual from Barcelona tells me why Italian pipes are the most beautiful pipes ever made. I feel the same way when Tad Gage explains why no pipes can compare with old Barling pipes. Years ago, I was excited to hear Basil Sullivan talk enthusiastically about his Charatan collection and Edsel James about his Dunhill collection. Talk about a lifelong love affair with their pipes!

Along the same lines, I always want to buy another Jim Cooke pipe after Bob Noble waxes poetic about them, and I love it when Tom Looker tells us about Tokutomi, Teddy and other pipe sculptors. I grew to appreciate Tracy Mincer and Custombilt pipes after reading Bill Unger's fine book about them, and I was so impressed by Neill Archer Roan's descriptions of North American pipe artisans, such as Jeff Gracik and Todd Johnson, that I started buying their pipes.

This is what makes the hobby fun for all of us.

Now there are some collectors who consider themselves "experts," and who might criticize your choices. But how can someone else be an "expert" on what you like?

It drives me nuts when I read attacks on individual pipe makers and pipe brands. I believe we are too small a community to sustain a climate of petty criticism, where some people try to score debating points at the expense of others, and I refuse to participate when these conversations start to develop.

I believe it is a mistake to over-analyze the art of pipe smoking. Some collectors remind me of the old joke in which two psychiatrists pass each other when they arrive at work and one says, "Good morning," and the other turns to a colleague and says, "I wonder what he meant by that." Yes, I have known some collectors who really were that suspicious.

While it is true that our palates can become more sophisticated over time as pipe smokers, it becomes dangerous when experienced collectors conclude they have superior abilities over the rest of us that allow them to enjoy their tobacco smoke better than we can. Picture two guys in a restaurant eating hamburgers, and one says to the other, "I can taste my hamburger better than you can taste yours." That kind of thinking is not only elitist, it is silly.

My advice is to run a hundred miles from anyone who espouses pipe collecting dogma. There are people in all walks of life, including pipe collecting, who have a knack for taking something fun and making it un-fun, for taking a pleasant experience and making it unpleasant.

Be aware of the fact that some collectors are simply not satisfied with enjoying their own pipes. They need to put down other pipes in order to feel important. But as my friend John Goldberg says, "if you really don't like a pipe, then really don't buy it."

And please, watch out for personal attacks. There is no place for them in the hobby. We can disagree on a number of issues, but there is no reason to be disagreeable or to name names in a game of one-upmanship.

But remember, all of these practices are only dangerous if you pay attention to them.

What I find much more rewarding is to pay attention to truly knowledgeable collectors who genuinely love the hobby. One of the best examples is longtime friend Rich Esserman of the New York Pipe Show. Rich and I have discussed these topics over the years, and his insights are invaluable. For instance, he points out that Alfred Dunhill's famous book is called, "The Gentle Art of Smoking," with emphasis on the word "art."

It is a mistake to look for scientific principles in matters that boil down to personal taste. We all agree that as you become more experienced and knowledgeable, your tastes can change. But for Rich, the important point is to have an open dialogue about what pipe brands smoke well -- for him and for you.

Rich and I recently corresponded about these issues, and he wrote, "As with any discussion involving matters of taste and judgment, I accept the fact that someone else's taste might be completely different from my own, but that does not stop me from participating in the enjoyment of others." That is a great approach to the hobby because it is so positive and encouraging.

It is consistent with Mr. Dunhill's use of the word "gentle" in the title of his book. I have no doubt that the legendary pipe man is turning over in his grave because of the open hostility and vitriol we occasionally encounter, especially on the Internet, from a handful of unhappy collectors.

I suspect you are like me in that your reason for being a pipe smoker and pipe collector in the first place is to have a good time. Let me stress this point by asking a question: Why in the world are we here, if not to have a good time? There is no other possible reason. So it is very much in our interest to block out all the silliness and focus instead on the things that we most like and enjoy about the hobby.

This is what I do today, and it is what I have tried to do ever since I smoked my first pipe bowl more than three decades ago. In fact, my only reason for getting involved in the pipe world is to have fun. I don't do it to make money, or to persuade people to adopt my point of view. I have been called a propagandist, but that is not accurate.

What I am is an enthusiastic collector who is eager to tell you what I like, and to hear about what you like. This is what was meant by the old expression, "The Brotherhood of the Briar."

Tell me all the great things about your pipes, and you will find an enthusiastic listener. Show me your latest acquisition, and you will find an admiring friend.

The International Committee of Pipe Clubs has a great slogan that they plaster all over their pipe shows and literature: "Relax with your pipe." That phrase captures the spirit and essence of a positive approach to pipe collecting.

Many of us find it exciting to learn as much as possible about pipes, not for the sake of science or some abstract concept of "truth," but for the sake of our own pleasure and enjoyment.

Nothing is so appealing as a group of people who are having a good time, who are enjoying one another's company. There is no better way to draw in new collectors than if they see that we are having a ball!

This hobby should be a never-ending source of fun and satisfaction, and it will be, if we approach our pipe collecting with a youthful, enthusiastic attitude of acceptance and optimism.

~~ BONUS CHAPTERS ~~

~~~~~

CHAPTER FIFTEEN

MAIL IT IN ONE PIECE, PLEASE

On the bottom is a pipe by Adam Davidson that should be sent as one piece to preserve the flush fit, while the pipe on top, by Lars Ivarsson, can be sent as two pieces because the silver ring will prevent the wood from expanding and contracting. Still, my own preference is to send all pipes in one piece.

This was an article that I wrote for pipesmagazine.com, and several pipe sellers expressed disagreement, while others thanked me for explaining why I like to have pipes kept together when they are shipped long distances.

A perfectly flush finish on a pipe is rare, but it is one of those finer points of craftsmanship that can mean a great deal to the connoisseur.

* * * * *

It was a Saturday afternoon in Los Angeles, and I was in my garage with the great Danish pipe maker Jess Chonowitsch, showing him how I cleaned the inside of my pipes. We had three on a table, and I had separated all three -- meaning, pulled the mouthpiece out so that each pipe was in two pieces. Just as I brought down the alcohol and tube brushes that we were going to use for cleaning the pipes, my wife called out to say that lunch was ready.

I started to walk into the house, and Jess said, "We can't leave the pipes separated like that." I explained that we would be back in less than an hour, but he was concerned, saying that pipes should be held together as one piece except for very short periods of time. "Otherwise," he said, "the wood will expand or contract and you will lose your perfect fit."

Jess was talking about pipes with a stem that is flush with the shank, and by "perfect fit," he meant that the two appear to be inseparable when together. This was one of the first things I noticed about his pipes nearly two decades ago. A blind man running his finger along the mouthpiece and shank of a Jess Chonowitsch pipe could not tell which was rubber and which was wood -- they were seamless, as if one piece.

When you receive pipes in the mail, have you noticed how often the senders separate the mouthpiece from the pipe and send them as separate items in the same box? If it is a Peterson system pipe or any other military mount or push-pull type of mouthpiece, that is fine. But if it is a traditional flush-fitted pipe, I believe they should be sent as one piece. Otherwise, pipes with a perfect fit, if separated for shipping, arrive with a bump when they are put back together.

When I have asked pipe sellers why they separate the two before shipping, their explanation is that it is too dangerous, that the pipe is much more likely to break in shipping if it is connected as one piece.

However, if you use enough bubble wrap, the pipe is no more likely to break or be damaged, and the advantages are enormous.

The pipe makers I have written so much about over the years -- Lars Ivarsson, Jess Chonowitsch, Bo Nordh and S. Bang -- all send their pipes as one piece and have never had a problem.

In fact, Bo used to ask me not to separate the pipe after it arrived for at least three weeks and preferably six weeks.

This is because wood expands and contracts depending upon the temperature as well as the amount of humidity or dryness in the air.

If you ever get an old pipe that you are afraid to separate because the stem appears glued to the shank, just put it in a baggie in the freezer for a half hour and then slowly open it. The wood contracts in the freezer, which loosens the fit of the tenon in the mortise. When the wood contracts, it actually creates a larger space for the tenon to fit into. Thus, you will be able to open a previously-stuck pipe.

One time when I was at a ranch in Santa Barbara I had left a few pipes on a table for cleaning. They were separated and I got called away for several hours. This was before Jess taught me not to keep them apart for more than a few minutes at a time. They were separated for three or four hours in 90-degree heat that was incredibly dry, and when I tried to put the mouthpieces back together, it was very risky. I was afraid of cracking the shank. So I put beeswax on the tenons and gently twisted them together, but only after waiting until the outside temperature had cooled down quite a bit.

If you don't have beeswax around, just use a bar of soap. Ulf Noltensmeier of the S. Bang pipes gave me that tip, and I have used it many times in hotel rooms over the years. Just take the bar of soap and rub a little on the tenon. You don't need much, and a little bit on two sides of the tenon will do the trick.

Have you ever had your fingers swell up and found it difficult to get your wedding ring off? The solution is to wash your hands with soap so that your finger becomes slippery and the ring slides off much more easily.

I remember once flying from Chicago to Miami in January, when it was 10 degrees below zero in Chicago when I got on the plane, and 90-plus degrees in Miami when I got off the plane. I distinctly remember that my wedding ring practically fell off my finger in Chicago, while I needed soap and water to get it off in Miami. Heat expands matter.

Have you ever taken your shoes off during a flight and then had difficulty putting them back on because your feet have swollen so much? Imagine what is happening to any pipes that might also be on that flight!

Todd Johnson, the talented American pipe maker, once showed me how water can expand the wood inside the shank by applying a teardrop of water to the mortise area on a pipe with a loose-fitting stem. After waiting for a minute or two, for the water to dry, he then put the mouthpiece together with the pipe, and the fit was tight.

Prior to that, if I had a loose-fitting stem, I would heat the tenon and then, when it was warm, gently press it against a firm surface to expand the tenon so it would fit. But I much prefer Todd's way of adding a teardrop of water to the shank. It is so natural, and it does not require permanently expanding the tenon.

I corresponded with Todd about this article, and he mentioned that he prefers Delrin tenons. I know of other pipe makers who have used Delrin, including Jess Chonowitsch and Jeff Gracik. Speaking as a customer, I much prefer that material too. As Todd says, "With Delrin there is more 'fudge' room for the mortise to expand and contract."

Todd characterized the practice of separating the pipe into two pieces as something that "is ALWAYS a foolish endeavor. If things change--expand or contract--you want them to change TOGETHER!" He also pointed out that he does not want for his pipes to arrive with a note saying, "some assembly required."

I realize that many old estate pipes have a bump -- a slightly raised ridge where the shank meets the mouthpiece -- so it's probably not that big a deal to send them as two pieces. But with all the new artisan pipes being made today, I hope that sellers of their pipes will keep them together for shipment.

A related problem occurs if the pipe maker rushes the process, if he makes the pipe and ships it out before the tenon has had a chance to sit in the shank for a few weeks. That is why pipe makers like Jess and Bo always had a dozen half-finished pipes on their work benches at a time. They were letting the wood dry out and form as one with the mouthpiece.

There is a further problem -- an explanation for why some of the newer artisan pipes lack a flush finish -- which is that the pipe makers are using wood that has not dried out completely. That is a much more complicated problem.

However, when I buy a new pipe that has a perfect flush finish, I try not to separate the stem for at least several months, and never for more than a few minutes at a time. I have found that by being cautious at the beginning, the smooth transition between rubber and wood will be preserved for many years.

But the starting point is to make certain that these pipes are sent in the mail as one piece, not two.

~~~~~

CHAPTER SIXTEEN

PIPES AND POLITICS

The North American Indians introduced the *peace pipe* for a reason, and we should follow their lead.

North American Indians made the peace pipe famous. These were long, decorated ceremonial pipes that typically were smoked as a token of peace, especially after the settlement of a dispute.

If you are a pipe smoker in the 21st century, always keep that image in mind ... and avoid getting into political debates with your pipe friends! You'll never settle anything, and it's just not worth it.

At the same time, try to be aware of the hostility to smoking (as if that needs any effort.) as a decided change in the world today. This is what all pipe smokers have to live with, but we value our pipe smoking so much that it just goes with the territory. If you are a pipe smoker, then I hope your philosophy is to live and let live.

* * * * *

In 1977, I was a Baltimore-based reporter for United Press International, aged 27, and just starting to experiment with pipe smoking. I was on the phone with a government official who had issued a press release talking about "ETS," which stood for Environmental Tobacco Smoke, the precursor to what we now call secondhand smoke.

After he explained his official position, we started chatting, and he asked me if I smoked. I said yes, but I was giving up cigarettes because I could feel the damage to my health, and I was experimenting with the pipe. He countered that abstinence was my only choice.

"We're not going to let you walk around with a little cloud over your head," he said.

I thought, *"We're not going to let you?!?* Who's not going to let me? Who the hell are you to tell me what to do?"

Since I was representing UPI, I bit my tongue, though I cannot stress how stunned I was by his comment. In America, you will tell me I cannot smoke my pipe?

But his mentality from 35 years ago has become the norm today. It represents a way of governing that has since been labeled the "nanny state," and it is now accepted by far too many people in America, where the mayor of New York has prohibited the sale of soft drinks in extra large containers.

When pipe smokers adopt this same mentality, I think of the Stockholm Syndrome, the psychological experience in which victims start defending their captors.

Smoking has been banned at many pipe shows, and a growing number of attendees are praising the ban.

"I like the clean air," or "My eyes no longer burn," or "Finally I can breath at a show," or "You don't need to shoot a gun at a gun show," or "This is much healthier," or whatever.

All of these comments would have been unfathomable 20 years ago, or even up until the last 10 years.

Now I realize that some of this is simply making the best of a bad situation, and many of the pipe smokers who like the smoke-free shows still oppose these bans on political grounds.

But my bigger complaint is that society has told us that our pipe smoke is bothering them, and many of us have accepted this unconsciously and then sided with the antis. That is why we are so shocked when see all that smoking in the TV series *Mad Men*. (However, some of us are old enough to remember that that is exactly how it was. In fact, before becoming a reporter I was a copy writer at the Leo Burnett advertising agency and saw that world firsthand, including routine smoking in the elevator.)

In the latest Sherlock Holmes series on Masterpiece Mystery, we see a "three pipe problem" changed to a "three patch problem," in which the 21st century Sherlock shows us three nicotine patches on his arm. They are on his forearm, just where a heroin junkie would inject needles. Compare that with Arthur Conan Doyle's portrait of the real Sherlock Holmes using his pipe for meditation as he was solving yet another mystery.

When I started smoking a pipe, and collecting pipes, my friends and mentors were invariably the type of people who wanted to be left alone to enjoy their pipes and their lives. We rarely talked about politics, but when we did, I don't ever remember disagreeing or being offended.

During the past decade there has been a pretty sizable shift in the perspective of people I meet at pipe shows. There is an in-your-face attitude at times that I find extremely offensive. For a while I stopped visiting a certain pipe store that I used to enjoy because the conversations too often switched from pipes to politics, and I frequently found myself in the minority, being lectured to, when I simply wanted to relax with my pipe.

At the height of the 2012 presidential election I was talking to a young pipe enthusiast, and we made the mistake of shifting our conversation from pipes to politics. I said that I did not know much about one of the candidates, but, from what I had seen, I liked his message.

My young friend disliked that candidate, claiming that he was a phony, or some such thing. I said that all politicians have to lie to some extent to get elected, and he replied, "Yes, but your side lies better than mine."

I told him that was really an offensive statement, and he apologized, saying it was only a joke. As it turns out, I like this young man, but we have agreed to avoid discussing politics in the future.

How about the European pipe makers? Is it different there?

I remember once joining some Italian pipe makers at a Sunday breakfast at the Chicago Pipe Show, and several of them got into a heated argument in Italian. The fellow sitting next to me whispered, "That one is a communist and the other one is for capitalism."

Many of us have heard European pipe makers tell us how wonderful their socialist governments are and then ask us to pay cash for their pipes so they can avoid paying taxes -- astronomical taxes, by the way.

There is one European pipe maker who is adamantly anti-smoking, saying, "I would never smoke a pipe -- it is much too unhealthy."

There has been a change in the hobby, all right, and if you are one of those who wants to tell me that you won't let me live my life with a little cloud over my head, using the words of that government bureaucrat from 35 years ago, I would tell you to stuff it. But that would be impolite, so I will just tell you to leave me alone to enjoy my pipes, and let's avoid discussing politics altogether.

Epilogue

~ ~ ~ ~ ~

Pipe Dreams Realized

By Tad Gage

Faced with prevalent anti-tobacco sentiment these days, it is sometimes discouraging to be an avid pipe smoker. A reminder of why we do what we do can go a long way to invigorating the spirit. This very readable, well-written book accomplishes that. I believe it will inspire you, as it did me, to keep the faith in spite of the obstacles being tossed in our paths.

The irony is that when Rick Newcombe first asked me to write the epilogue, he barely let me get a word in edgewise before he explained his request. I chuckled, because I already had a pretty good idea what he wanted to say. I let him explain anyway. After I read "Still Searching for Pipe Dreams," his rationale perfectly summed up the spirit of this engaging and quietly rebellious book.

Rick and I have known each other a long time. Sadly, our geographic distance (Rick is on the West Coast and I live in Chicago) afford us few opportunities to see each other. But that is no different than the situation with the pipe friends we've both made over the years, some who live a few miles from us and others who live a few thousand miles away. But through our writings, emails, Internet or phone conversations, and our all-too-infrequent personal meetings, we understand each others' affinity for pipes and those who smoke them.

Rick and I have different preferences in the pipes we collect and prefer to smoke. He primarily smokes new pipes created by "modern day" pipe makers. Because it's possible to buy and smoke pipes more than 150 years old, I should say my interpretation of "modern day" means a pipe made during the past 50 years! On the other hand, I primarily collect, smoke and thoroughly enjoy pipes made by Benjamin Barling & Sons, a five-generation English company that operated from 1812 to 1962.

If Rick and I were typical collectors with such divergent tastes (for example, in automobiles or antique furniture), you might think our interests were radically different and we would have little in common. Pipe collecting is something unique, giving us the freedom to share the commonalities and be stimulated by the differences, while still being united by our love of all things related to pipes.

Rick, for instance, has owned, smoked and greatly enjoyed many of the old English pipe brands I dearly love. And I own any number of new or "newer" creations, and I enjoy these pipes immensely! I have a treasured set of matched grain crosscut horns made for me by master American carver Jim Cooke, cut yin-yang from the same block of briar he waited five years to find. One features his renowned sandblast (which runs parallel to the pipe instead of the usual ring grain blast) and a smooth birdseye and cross-grain (which Jim affectionately calls a "second" because almost all his pipes feature his exquisite sandblasting technique).

Although Rick's and my pipe collections diverge in age and makers, we both tend to prefer traditional shapes like billiards. Still, we both admire more free-form pipe creations, and we understand and appreciate the reason many pipe smokers favor these artistic shapes.

Rick and I also share many preferences in the pipe tobaccos we enjoy in our similar but dissimilar pipes – another and completely different layer of camaraderie because we can completely separate the tobaccos we enjoy from the pipes in which we enjoy them. Beyond that is the level of a satisfying personal interaction. Coming from different backgrounds, professions and places, Rick and I would never have met without our shared affinity for the pipe. Pipe smoking and collecting has been the binding agent between people of varying tastes, interests, professions, ages, economic levels and geographic locations.

So back to my original tease: why did Rick feel a need to explain why he asked me to pen an introduction? Simply out of respect that, as pipe collectors, we do indeed have different preferences. He found that difference intriguing, and so did I! As you'll discover when reading his book, those differences are not a reason for division, but a chance to celebrate our diversity (an overused word these days, but I think it fits).

Rick's writings cover a gamut of anecdotes and observations about the delights of pipes and tobaccos. More than that, his essays convey how pipes and tobaccos act as a mortar that binds us pipe collectors together. At many points in the book I nodded in agreement with his observations about this beloved "brotherhood (and sisterhood) of the pipe." The warm recollections of an evening meal with pipe friends, the enervating feeling of a lively all-night conversation at a pipe show, or the simple, peaceful moments of solitary reflection at home with a favorite pipe filled with well-aged and carefully blended tobacco.

I'd like to share one personal story because it not only dovetails with something Rick has written about, but also illustrates why pipe smoking and collecting is about the pipes, but also so much more.

In Rick's essay "Is It All In My Head?," he discusses the birth of what many consider to be the grandfather of all the freehand pipes we see, smoke and enjoy today – an unusual cornucopia horn-shaped pipe created by master carver Sixten Ivarsson in the late 1950s that required considerable hand work because of the unusual angles. That shape has given birth to many never-before-seen pipe shapes that couldn't be cranked out on a lathe in a factory.

I owned such a pipe for many years as part of my small collection of freehand horn-shaped pipes crafted by Danish, German and American pipe makers. The shape is one I have an affinity for, and is radically different than most of the standard shaped pipes I own. It was hand-made by Sixten in 1964 (date-stamped and with the cost in Danish kroners also stamped in the pipe) – a very early example of the original freehand pipe. It is a remarkable horn with two parallel panels on each side. The top and bottom of this sweeping creation are pure birdseye, while the sides are identical sunbursts of straight grain.

I cherished it as a great smoker and a work of art until, at one of the Chicago International Pipe Collector shows Rick so frequently mentions, I had a conversation with Rex Poggenpohl, a renowned collector of Danish freehands who was displaying some of his most interesting pieces as part of the show's educational exhibits. Turns out Rex had structured the glass-encased exhibit as a "family tree" of great Danish freehands, showing their evolution over the decades. When I pulled out the pipe, which I brought to the show to smoke and with no intent of selling, guess what? The ONE pipe missing from the display was, indeed, the grandfather of all freehands.

We reached an accord on what we both felt was a fair price, and for the remainder of the show, I proudly saw my former pipe at the apex of the display cabinet. Something like the "Lucy" pipe equivalent to the evolution of human beings! I miss that pipe, but I know it found an even better home. Many of us pipe collectors experience that emotion when selling or trading a cherished pipe, because they really are our "old friends." I own numerous pipes that were loved by their former owners, sold to me on the one condition that "I know you will enjoy it even more than I, and it belongs in your collection, but if you ever decide to sell it, I have first dibs on buying it back." And so it goes.

Many of you will be reading this as an e-book, and you should know Rick and I are all for technology. It's today's reality. We're not old farts who spend a lot of time yearning for the old days of tube televisions and rabbit ear antennae, Edsels and manual typewriters. But there are times when the hectic, crazed, information-overload, 24/7, stressed-out, plugged-in, turned-on pace of today's lifestyle must sometimes be cowed into submission: if not with a 10-foot pole, then with a six inch briar.

Rick's writings remind us that pipes are much more than objects. They help define us, comfort us, invigorate us and bring us together; like the indelible image of the ritual sharing of the Native American peace pipe or even today's craze for communal hookah smoking. I hope Rick's observations and his passion for the pastime contribute to encouraging veteran pipe smokers to appreciate what they have, even in the face of constant bombardment of anti-tobacco sentiment, and to inspire a new generation of pipe smokers.

As Rick eloquently noted: "Pipe smoking requires a rebellious spirit." Indeed, it may be a quiet, peaceful and even contemplative rebellion. But it is a rebellion nonetheless: to preserve something as primal and human as putting flame to leaf in a container fashioned of wood, clay, cob or meerschaum. That is a rebellion of which I am proud to be a participant.

ACKNOWLEDGMENTS AND CREDITS

So many people have offered so much encouragement since I started writing about pipes more than 30 years ago, beginning with a profile of Baltimore tobacconist Bill Fader in 1977, that I find it very easy to write about all aspects of pipe collecting that I enjoy. I want to thank and acknowledge some of the individuals who have supported my efforts, starting with the editors of pipe magazines who published some of the articles that appear in this book, especially Bill Unger of The Pipe Collector, Chuck Stanion of Pipes and Tobaccos, Kevin Godbee of pipesmagazine.com, and the late Tom Dunn of The Pipe Smoker's Ephemeris.

I also want to thank the show organizers who invited me to speak at their pipe show dinners, since some of those speeches became various chapters of this book. They include Matt Guss for the Seattle dinner, Robert Vance for the Los Angeles dinner, Steve O'Neill and Marty Pulvers for the West Coast Pipe Show dinner and Craig Cobine and Frank Burla for the Chicago talk.

Marianne Sugawara and I have worked together for more than 20 years, and, as a result, she has learned much more about pipes than she ever wanted to know. She also has become friends with Jess Chonowitsch and other people in the pipe business. It was Marianne who made it possible for me to see exactly what each chapter would look like in book form. Since I am a visual person, this was absolutely essential for these writings to actually become a book, and I simply could not have done this without her.

I want to thank Tad Gage for his Epilogue. Tad and I first met too many years ago to count, and, as he points out, I thought it would show the diversity of pipe collecting by having him -- whose collecting interests are totally different from mine -- write his thoughts and reflections about the book. Yes, as Tad says, regardless of specialties, we pipe smokers are all in this rebellion together.

As for photo credits, I want to thank the

following: The cover photo of a beautiful Lars Ivarsson pipe was taken by Adrienne Harrell and provided by Sykes Wilford of smokingpipes.com. John Rockwell, son of the late artist, granted me permission to reprint Norman Rockwell's "Triple Self-Portrait." Vernon Vig helped me find just the right photo for Chapter 2, which was taken by Henryk Rogalski of Poland. The photos for Chapters 5 and 6, and both photos on the back cover, are courtesy of Robert Gardner Studios in Los Angeles. The photo for Chapter 7 was taken by John Sutherland, and the photos for Chapter 8 were taken, in order, by Carole Newcombe, Dayton Matlick and Jan Hängsel, the last one being provided by Jan Andersson. The photo for Chapter 10 came from Jeff Gracik, Chapter 11 from Robert Newcombe, Chapter 12 was a photo taken by a friendly tourist with a camera phone who shot the picture at my request when I spotted that unusual men's restroom sign in China, and Chapter 13 was courtesy of Nanna Ivarsson. Tad Gage sent me his photo for the Epilogue.

As for the close-up of my face at the start of Chapter 14, there was an interesting story behind it. Carole and I were visiting Helsinki, Finland in October 2011, on the same trip that I wrote about in Chapter 13. One morning after walking around the city, we found a comfortable park bench at a city square. We were watching youthful Swedish soccer fans whoop and holler on behalf of their country's team in advance of a big game against Finland that night.

Just then a young lady approached us and asked if she could take our picture. Her name was Roosa Jakosaari, and she explained that she was in a photography class with an assignment to go out into the city and find interesting-looking people to photograph. She said they had to be total strangers. After she took a few pictures, I pulled out a pipe, and she smiled enthusiastically and said, "Yes!" and snapped the tightly-cropped photo that you see on Page 154.

Made in the USA
Columbia, SC
06 February 2025

53368725R00100